THE SOMERSET and DORSET JOINT RAILWAY

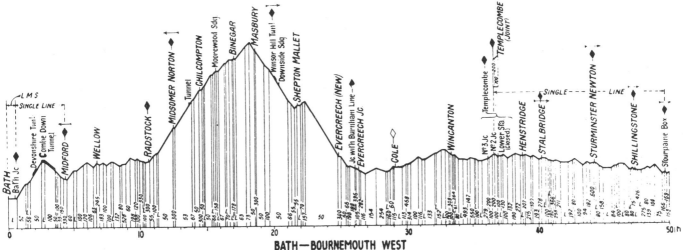

BATH—BOURNEMOUTH WEST

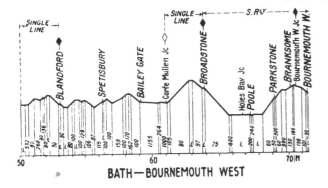

BATH—BOURNEMOUTH WEST

gradient profiles by permission of The Railway Magazine.

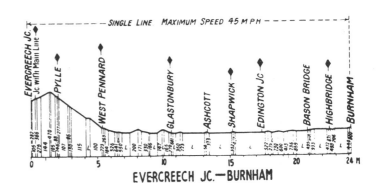

SINGLE LINE MAXIMUM SPEED 45 M.P.H.

EVERCREECH JC.—BURNHAM

A delightful feature of the Somerset and Dorset—the wide variety and contrast in locomotives used over the line.

The down "Pines Express" climbs towards Midsomer Norton hauled by one of O.V.S. Bulleid's Southern Pacifics, No. 34093 "Saunton", built in 1949, and assisted by 3F 0-6-0 No. 43216, built for the S & D.J.R. in 1902 to a Midland design by S.W. Johnson.

1st August, 1953

The Somerset and Dorset in the 'Fifties

PART 1

1950~1954

One of the classic scenes on the Somerset and Dorset—
an up express setting off from Evercreech Junction.

This was the scene on 12th July, 1952, as 2P 4-4-0 No. 40697 and 7F 2-8-0 No. 53800, with twelve on, made their dramatic departure from the Junction. Ahead of them lay the gruelling ascent of the Mendips—8½ miles, much of it at 1 in 50, up to Masbury Summit, 811 feet above sea level. The climbing started immediately, right from the platform end. No wonder there were never any 'half measures' when setting off north from Evercreech Junction!

The
Somerset and Dorset
in the 'Fifties

PART 1
1950~1954

by

Ivo Peters B.E.M.

GUILD PUBLISHING LONDON

S & D 7F No. 53808 on Bath shed after her return from Derby with a small boiler.

16th January, 1954

S & D 7F No. 53809 emerges from Devonshire Tunnel with a down goods.

15th March, 1952

THE TWO PRESERVED SOMERSET AND DORSET 7F 2-8-0s

To the great delight of all admirers of these splendid engines, two S & D 7F 2-8-0s have been preserved.

No. 53808 is owned by the Somerset and Dorset Railway Museum Trust, and is being restored at the Trust's headquarters at Washford, on the West Somerset Railway.

No. 53809 was saved from the scrapyard by Mr. Frank Beaumont who purchased the engine for preservation. This 7F is being meticulously restored by Mr. Beaumont and a group of four volunteers, and the present intention is for the engine to go to the Midland Railway Trust at Butterley, in Derbyshire.

This edition published 1986 by
Book Club Associates
by arrangement with
Oxford Publishing Co.

Printed in Great Britain by
Biddles Ltd., Guildford and Kings Lynn

The train times quoted throughout this book are from the Working Time Table. (SO) after a train time indicates that the train ran only on Saturdays during the summer service.

ACKNOWLEDGEMENTS

In putting together "The Somerset and Dorset in the 'Fifties" I have had the good fortune to have the unstinting help and advice of several of my friends. The printing of the photographs was done by Derek Mercer and Peter Skelton both of whom went to great trouble to get the best possible prints from my ageing S & D negatives. My old friend Peter Smith, one time engineman on the Somerset and Dorset, read through my manuscript and in addition to giving me much useful information, also corrected several mistakes which had crept in! Once again, Peggy Leitch has deciphered my illegible handwriting, and typed out my manuscript, and my sister Luise Girdlestone has happily taken on her usual tedious task of checking the proofs. As with all my books, Angela O'Shea has been of immense help with her constructive criticism of my picture arrangements and the phrasing of the captions. To all these friends who have given me so much help, I am most grateful.

Finally, I wish to express my very sincere appreciation to my publisher, Colin Judge, for allowing me to do my own picture arrangements and layouts. With O.P.C., if, for example, there is a fir tree in the left hand side of one of my photographs—then that fir tree will definitely be in the reproduced picture!

An up goods, hauled by 7F No. 53802, draws near to Moorewood.

21st March, 1953

INTRODUCTION

The 1950s was a fascinating period in the history of the Somerset and Dorset, and one of outstanding interest for the railway enthusiast. At the start of the decade, the S & D was flourishing. Considerable freight was being handled by the line and, with cars hard to come by after the recent World War, many people were travelling by train.

Bournemouth, the delightful resort on the South Coast, was becoming increasingly popular with people in the Midlands and the North of England for their summer holidays, and passenger traffic over the Somerset and Dorset on summer Saturdays was reaching remarkable figures.

A study of the 1950 Working Time Table will show the number of regular through passenger trains being run on summer Saturdays. In addition to these, at the height of the holiday season—the last weekend in July and the first weekend in August—many extra trains were run from such diverse places as Coventry, Derby, Rose Grove, Walsall, Leicester, Kidsgrove, and Preston, just to mention a few. By the early 'fifties this summer weekend traffic had reached such proportions that on several occasions, every S & D engine that

could turn a wheel, had to be pressed into service. Bournemouth Motive Power Depot also came to the rescue with liberal lending of engines, and in addition, from Thursday evenings onwards, any suitable 'foreign' engine arriving on Bath shed after working in from the North, would be quietly tucked away behind the water softening plant, and then 'borrowed' for the weekend before being sent back home on the following Monday!

The Somerset and Dorset was always an interesting line from the motive power angle, although prior to the Second World War, there had not been much variety in the types of locomotives used. But in the 1950s, due in part to responsibility for motive power being transferred from the London Midland Region to the Southern Region and then finally to the Western Region of British Railways, a wide and constantly changing variety of engines ran over the line. At the start of the 'fifties, the London Midland Region was responsible for S & D motive power, and set out overleaf is the official list of engines allocated to the Somerset and Dorset line as at 1st September, 1950.

This book, which is the first of two volumes on the Somerset and Dorset in the 'fifties, covers the five years from 1950 to 1954.

Ivo Peters
1980

2P No. 509 and 'Black Five' No. 44839 leaving Winsor Hill Tunnel with the down "Pines Express".

4th March, 1950

Class 4F 0-6-0 No. 44560.

Class 2P 4-4-0 No. 40700

Class 5MT 4-6-0 No. 44839.

Class 7F 2-8-0 No. 53804.

Class 3F 0-6-0 No. 43419.

Class 3F 0-6-0T No. 47275.

Class 0F 0-4-0ST No. 51202.

Class 1P 0-4-4T No. 58047.

Class 4MT 2-6-0 No. 43017.

Class 2MT 2-6-2T No. 41243.

ALLOCATION OF ENGINES, SOMERSET AND DORSET MOTIVE POWER DEPOTS

1st September, 1950

BATH (and sub-shed RADSTOCK)

Class 2P 4-4-0	Class 5MT 4-6-0	Class 3F 0-6-0T
568	44826	47275
569	44830	7316
40601	44839	47465
40696	44945	7496
40697	45440	7542
40698		47557
40700		

Class 2MT 2-6-2T	Class 4F 0-6-0	Class 7F 2-8-0
41240	43875	53800
41241	44096	53801
41242	44235	53802
41243	44422	53803
	44523	53804
Class 4MT 2-6-0	44535	53805
43013	44557	53806
43017	44558	53807
43036	44559	53808
	44560	53809
Class 0F 0-4-0ST	44561	53810
51202		

Sentinel
7191

TEMPLECOMBE

Class 2P 4-4-0	Class 3F 0-6-0	Class 4F 0-6-0
40505	43194	44102
509	43216	44146
40563	43218	44417
40564	43228	
40634	43248	
	43356	

HIGHBRIDGE

Class 1P 0-4-4T	Class 3F 0-6-0
58046	43204
58047	43419
58086	43792
58088	

1. In 1950 the 2P 4-4-0 and Stanier 'Black Five' 4-6-0 were the mainstay of motive power for passenger trains on the Somerset and Dorset main line. 2P No. 40601 and 'Black Five' No. 44830 are standing at the coal stage prior to moving off shed to work the down "Pines Express". Note the breakdown crane in the background. In 1950 a breakdown train was permanently stabled at Bath.

6th May, 1950

1950

The London Midland Region was responsible for Somerset & Dorset motive power, having inherited this role from the L.M.S. when the railways of Britain were nationalised in 1948. S & D motive power depots came under Bristol (London Midland Region), their shed codes being Bath 22C, Templecombe 22D, Highbridge 22E. (Radstock was a sub-shed of Bath, and Branksome became a sub-shed of Templecombe in February, 1950.)

This was the situation prevailing at the beginning of 1950, but there was soon to be a change, for in February, responsibility for Somerset & Dorset motive power was transferred to the Southern Region. S & D sheds now came under Eastleigh, the new codes being—Bath 71G, Templecombe 71H, Highbridge 71J.

Initially, the locomotive stock remained unchanged, the entire stud being on loan from the London Midland Region.

2. Mr. Arthur Elliott, the Bath shedmaster—or shed foreman as the appointment was known in 1950. Mr. Elliott was a strict disciplinarian, and during his 'reign' at Bath M.P.D., everyone on the depot was kept very much on his toes.

3. 7F 2-8-0 No. 53804 starts to ease forward for the run up to the S & D goods yard from where she would shortly be setting off with the 12.35 p.m. Bath–Evercreech Junction freight.

The two black tanks behind the engine were installed for oil storage, but never used. The government's grandiose scheme for converting to oil firing large numbers of locomotives on the newly nationalised railways, came to an abrupt end when it was found there was not the foreign currency available to pay for the oil.

25th February, 1950

At the beginning of the 'fifties, freight traffic on the main line was in the very capable hands of the S & D 7F 2-8-0s. Trains on the Branch were worked mainly by S.W. Johnson's 3F 0-6-0s and 1P 0-4-4 tanks.

4. Johnson 0-4-4T No. 58047, and her fireman, take a rest at Evercreech Junction. Having run in off the branch with the 9.45 a.m. train from Burnham-on-Sea, No. 58047 had then propelled her train backwards out of the station and into the middle road, so as to free the down platform for the 9.00 a.m. (SO) from Bristol (9.48 a.m. off Bath).

12th August, 1950

5. Two S & D 7F 2-8-0s standing outside the Midland shed at Bath—No. 53805 (small boilered 1914 series) and No. 53806 (large boilered 1925 series).

7th August, 1950

THE SOMERSET AND DORSET
7F 2-8-0s

The original six locomotives of this class, designed by Sir Henry Fowler, were built at the Derby Works of the Midland Railway Company in 1914. They had boilers of 4 ft. $9^{1}/_{8}$ in. diameter, and were arranged for right hand drive. Their boiler pressure of 190 lb./sq. in., 21 in. diameter cylinders, and coupled wheels of 4 ft. 7½ in.,* produced a tractive effort of 35,932 lb. and made them the most powerful two-cylinder 2-8-0s in the country. On nationalisation of the railways in 1948, these six engines were allocated the numbers 53800 to 53805.

6.

In 1925 a further five locomotives were built at Darlington by Robert Stephenson and Company. This batch had larger boilers of 5 ft. 3 in. diameter and were arranged for left hand drive, resulting in the ejector gear being on the left hand side of the smokebox. Their British Railways numbers were 53806 to 53810.

In 1950 all eleven members of the class were going strong and giving excellent service. Two of the 1925 series had been rebuilt pre-war with the smaller boiler of 4 ft. $9^{1}/_{8}$ in. diameter, but 53806, 53807 and 53808 still retained larger diameter boilers and their own distinctive appearance.

*Increased to 4 ft. 8½ in. in the 'thirties when new tyres were fitted, which reduced slightly the tractive effort to 35,296 lb.

7.

In 1950 there were three variations in the front end of S & D 7F 2-8-0s—

6. No. 53805, one of the original batch, with small boiler and right hand drive.

7. No. 53806, one of the 1925 series, with large boiler and left hand drive. (Note ejector gear on left hand side of smokebox.)

8. No. 53810, a 1925 series engine rebuilt with a small diameter boiler, necessitating the insertion of a distance-piece in the smokebox saddle.

8.

9. No. 53803, 1914 series, with 4 ft 9¹⁄₈ in. diameter boiler (type G9AS).

10. No. 13806 (still carrying her pre-nationalisation number), 1925 series, with 5 ft. 3 in. diameter boiler (type G9BS).

11. The maker's plate of No. 53804.

12. The maker's plate of No. 53807.

13. The cab of No. 53809. Note left hand drive position of this 1925 series engine.

THE DEPENDABLE 2Ps

In theory, a 4-4-0 locomotive with 6 ft. 9 in. coupled wheels should have been far from suitable for a mountainous line like the Somerset and Dorset, with a ruling gradient of 1 in 50. But in practice, the 2Ps—including the older Midland type with 7 ft. 0½ in. coupled wheels—rendered yeoman service on the S & D for over 40 years.

14. (Above) 2P No. 40634—built for the S & D J R in 1928—and 'Black Five' No. 44839 leaving Combe Down Tunnel with the down "Pines Express".

3rd June, 1950

15. (Left) Fifteen minutes later, 2P No. 40564 emerged from Combe Down Tunnel into Horsecombe Vale and the sunshine, to drift down over Tucking Mill viaduct with the 3.40 p.m. (SO) Bath-Templecombe stopping train.

3rd June, 1950

THE 4Fs—THE MAIDS OF ALL WORK

16. Amongst the Somerset and Dorset's stud of 4F 0-6-0s were five engines built specially for the S & D J R by Armstrong Whitworth & Company in 1922. The B.R. numbers of these engines were 44557 to 44561. In difficult conditions, with squalls of rain driving across the open hillside, S & D 4Fs Nos. 44560 and 44557 are plodding uphill towards Shepton Mallet with a northbound express.

12th August, 1950

17. 4F No. 44422 and 'Black Five' No. 44945 coasting downhill out of Devonshire Tunnel with the up "Pines Express". Happily this 4F is still 'alive' and is being painstakingly restored by the North Staffordshire Railway Society.

8th August, 1950

THE SOMERSET AND DORSET'S JOHNSON 0-4-4 TANKS

At the beginning of the 'fifties, S.W. Johnson's 0-4-4 tanks were still handling most of the branch line passenger trains. In 1950 Highbridge M.P.D. had four of these attractive 'elderly ladies', Nos. 58046, 58047, 58086 and 58088. All these had been reboilered with the exception of 58047 which still retained a round topped firebox and Salter valves on the dome. (And also L.M.S. on her tank sides!)

18. No. 58086 takes water at Evercreech Junction after arriving with the 9.45 a.m. train from Burnham-on-Sea. The fireman, perched comfortably on the cab roof, keeps an eye on the water level, whilst a cooperative porter prepares to turn off the supply when given the word. (Typifying the friendly spirit which prevailed amongst all the staff on the S & D.)

16th September, 1950

19. The 9.45 a.m. from Burnham-on-Sea, this time hauled by No. 58047, drops down the bank at the approach to Evercreech Junction station.
12th August, 1950

RADSTOCK MOTIVE POWER

20. A line-up of Radstock engines—ex-L & Y 0-4-0ST No. 51202 and two 3F 0-6-0Ts Nos. 7496 and 7316.

25th February, 1950

Four 'Jinty' 0-6-0 tank engines were kept at Radstock, which was a sub-shed of Bath, for banking goods trains up to Masbury Summit and also for shunting the collieries in the area. Some colliery sidings could only be reached by passing under Tyning's bridge–known to S & D enginemen as "Marble Arch"–which had the very restricted clearance of only 10 ft. 10 in. from rail level to the roof of the arch and so effectively prevented the 'Jintys' from reaching these sidings. To cope with this situation, Radstock had two very small locomotives. In 1950 these were an ex-Lancashire & Yorkshire Railway 0-4-0 saddle tank No. 51202 and a four-wheeled, geared, chain drive Sentinel, No. 7191. The unorthodox design of the Sentinel included the positioning of the vertical boiler in the cab which, except in the depth of winter, became absolutely stifling. So it was really no wonder that most Radstock enginemen preferred the little ex-L & Y 'Pug'.

21. Whenever I visited Radstock during 1950, the Sentinel was out of use, tucked away inside the shed. So that 7191 may be illustrated, my friend Dick Riley has kindly supplied this print of her. (A picture taken after she had acquired her B.R. number 47191.)

22.

The ex-L & Y 'Pug' standing ahead of two 'Jinty' 0-6-0 tanks. In the background is "Marble Arch" beneath which the 'Jintys' couldn't pass.

4th March, 1950

23. Ivatt class 4MT 2-6-0 No. 43017 on Bath shed. In this picture she is in original condition, with double blastpipe and chimney—the form in which these engines ran over the S & D in 1950.

2nd June, 1950

THE S & D's ENCOUNTER WITH THE IVATT CLASS 4MT 2-6-0s

By the beginning of the 'fifties, the Horwich mixed traffic class 5MT 2-6-0s—affectionately known as 'Crabs'—had disappeared from the S & D scene, and the Ivatt class 4MT 2-6-0s were in action (?) over the line. They had made their first appearance on the Somerset and Dorset in 1949, and in 1950 Bath M.P.D. had three of them, Nos. 43013, 43017 and 43036. The severity of the Somerset and Dorset line quickly sorted out the good from the indifferent in locomotive design, and it was not long before S & D enginemen found themselves in dire straits with their new 2-6-0s which just would not steam, however they were driven or fired. For 1950 the Somerset and Dorset was saddled with the Ivatt 2-6-0s, but then, much to the relief of the S & D enginemen—who had nicknamed the class 'Doodlebugs'—they quietly faded from the Somerset and Dorset scene.

Although not directly concerning the S & D, it is interesting to record that after a very detailed re-appraisal of the draughting of these locomotives, modifications were carried out which included the fitting of a single blastpipe and chimney in place of the original double arrangement. This transformed dramatically their performance and turned them into a good reliable class of locomotive.

24.
A rare sight on the S & D—two 'Doodlebugs' in double harness. Nos. 43017 and 43036, running over half an hour late, draw near to Binegar with the 10.35 a.m. (SO) Manchester to Bournemouth. For an amusing account of the trials and tribulations endured by the two footplate crews working this train, see Peter Smith's delightful book, "Footplate Over the Mendips" (page 90).

17th June, 1950

25. Ex-Midland 2P 4-4-0 No. 509 (which had not yet acquired her B.R. number) and Ivatt 4MT 2-6-0 No. 43017 climbing up past the grounds of Midford Castle with the 12.25 p.m. summer Saturday relief from Bournemouth to Birmingham.

5th August, 1950

26.

On a glorious afternoon in early August, 4F 0-6-0 No. 44417 and Ivatt 4MT 2-6-0 No. 43013 head south from Midford viaduct with the 10.35 a.m. (SO) Manchester to Bournemouth. There was not much doubt that long before Radstock had been reached, the 0-6-0 would be doing the major part of the work!

5th August, 1950

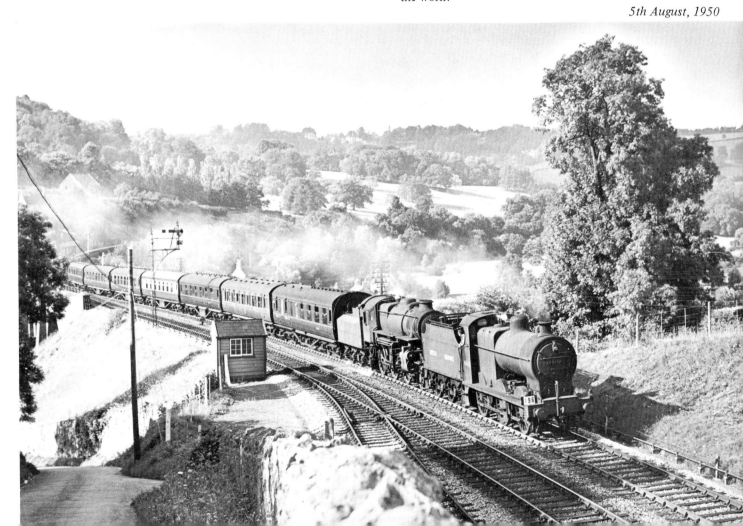

THE MOST INTERESTING EVENT OF THE YEAR— THE 7Fs START TO BE USED ON PASSENGER TRAINS

As the 1950 summer holiday season progressed, weekend traffic over the Somerset and Dorset line to Bournemouth grew rapidly until on the last Saturday in July the stage was reached where every S & D passenger and mixed traffic locomotive that was serviceable, was in use. With even more trains scheduled to run over the line on the following Saturday, 5th August, the situation became critical. The only motive power remaining available was the stud of eleven S & D 7F 2-8-0s—out and out freight locomotives, with 4 ft. 8½ in. coupled wheels, and no pretentions of being a mixed traffic type. But with the 'cupboard bare', Mr. Elliott, the Bath shedmaster, was left with no alternative but to authorise their restricted use on passenger trains—albeit with great reluctance and some foreboding.

27. Saturday, 5th August, 1950, saw the first rostered use of S & D 7F 2-8-0s on express passenger trains. In the event, on this first occasion only two 7Fs had to be used, one of which was No. 53804 seen here, assisted by 2P 4-4-0 No. 40698, climbing the bank out of Bath with the 7.33 a.m. (SO) Nottingham to Bournemouth.

5th August, 1950

28. (Above right) With 4F 0-6-0 No. 44235 coupled ahead of her, 7F 2-8-0 No. 53809 sets off from Bath with the 9.00 a.m. (SO) down semi-fast from Bristol to Bournemouth. The 4F was working down to Evercreech Junction to assist an up express over the Mendips later in the morning.

19th August, 1950

29. (Right) One of the many extra relief trains being run from Bournemouth on Saturday, 26th August, approaches Winsor Hill Tunnel, hauled by 2-6-2T No. 41240 and 7F 2-8-0 No. 53806. When 'Higher Authority' learnt about this particular combination of motive power, there were ructions! It was considered that with a small 2-6-2 tank coupled ahead of a heavy 7F 2-8-0, and the pair running fast downhill through the reverse curves on the northern slopes of the Mendips, there was a danger of buffer-locking. Instructions were issued forthwith that on no account was this combination to be used again! (I certainly never saw it happen a second time.)

26th August, 1950

30. On a lovely late afternoon in May, 7F No. 53810—one of the reboilered 1925 series—draws near to Binegar with the 3.45 p.m. down goods from Bath. The S & D had an interesting variety of signals. In this picture Binegar Distant—which is 'on'—had an upper quadrant arm mounted on a post made of two old rails bolted together. Moorewood Distant—which is 'off'—had an L & SWR lattice post and a lower quadrant arm.

30th May, 1950

BACK TO NORMAL! —7Fs on FREIGHT TRAINS

31. Large boilered 7F No. 53806 about to pass over Masbury Summit with the 11.20 a.m. Bath–Evercreech Junction freight.

11th November, 1950

32.

7F No. 53804—one of the original 1914 series—in charge of an up goods, prepares to do some shunting at Shepton Mallet. Next to the engine is an old S & DJR six-wheeled brake van. These vehicles were specially constructed at the Company's Highbridge Works for carrying the mail on the 2.40 a.m. down freight from Bath to Bournemouth. Although goods brake vans, they were built in the carriage shops, and incorporated such features as doors with carriage windows and locks.

Throughout its life, this train was always referred to by S & D staff as the '2.40 down Mail'. It certainly *did* carry the mail, but apart from this, was a normal goods train.

4th March, 1950

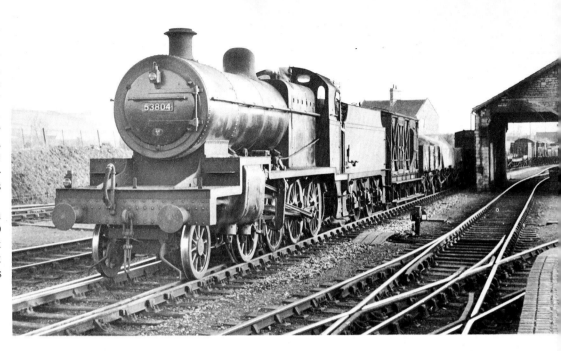

33. 7F No. 53809 climbing steadily southwards, emerges from the short, 66 yard long, Chilcompton Tunnel with the 5.15 p.m. Bath–Evercreech Junction goods. Happily, 53809 is still 'alive'. Most meticulously restored, she may be seen at The Midland Railway Trust, at Butterley, Derbyshire.

6th May, 1950

FREIGHT TRAFFIC OVER THE S & D

Considerable freight and minerals were being carried by the Somerset and Dorset in 1950, no less than twelve freight trains being scheduled to run from Bath to Evercreech Junction every day, except at weekends. In addition to normal goods traffic, large quantities of coal were carried from the collieries centred on Radstock and Midsomer Norton, and stone traffic from quarries in the Mendips was also substantial. To appreciate fully the extent of freight movements over the whole line, a study of the S & D Working Time Table for 1950 is highly recommended.

34. On a beautiful afternoon in early summer, without a cloud in the sky, 7F No. 53806—one of the large boilered 1925 series—is climbing towards Chilcompton Tunnel with the 3.45 p.m. down goods from Bath. This train was always referred to by S & D staff as "The Market", because it was scheduled to call at all stations between Radstock and Evercreech Junction.

13th May, 1950

35. Just over half an hour after taking the picture (above) of "The Market", 7F No. 53800, the doyen of the class, came on the scene with the 5.15 p.m. down goods. This was a through freight to Evercreech Junction and invariably a heavy train, necessitating banking assistance from Radstock up to Masbury Summit. A 'Jinty' 0-6-0T can just be seen at the rear of the train.

13th May, 1950

36. 7F No. 53810, in charge of an up goods, drifts out of Devonshire Tunnel and down the 1 in 50 bank into Bath.

8th August, 1950

37. The 12.35 p.m. down goods coming up the 1 in 50 bank out of Bath, hauled by large-boilered 7F No. 53806 and banked in the rear by a 4F 0-6-0.

8th August, 1950

EVERCREECH JUNCTION

One of the most interesting spots to be on the S & D on a summer Saturday—even in the rain!

38. From shortly after 10 a.m. on summer Saturdays, engines would start arriving and lining up in the middle road, ready to assist north bound expresses over the Mendips. Waiting in the middle road on a *very* wet Saturday morning in July were 2P 4-4-0 No. 40698, 4F 0-6-0 No. 44146 and 2P 4-4-0s Nos. 40696 and 568.

22nd July, 1950

39.
Stanier 'Black Five' No. 44839 stands in Evercreech Junction station with the down "Pines Express" on a miserable day of driving rain and near gale force wind. Whilst the class 5 took water, 2P No. 40634, which had given assistance from Bath over the Mendips, drew forward and then set back onto the up road, to get clear of 44839 before she resumed the run down to Bournemouth with the "Pines".

8th April, 1950

40. Sunshine for a change! In 1950 the only down express not scheduled to stop at Evercreech Junction, the 7.43 a.m. (SO) Birmingham to Bournemouth, approaches, drawn by 2P No. 40696 and 4F No. 44417. Standing in the middle road on the right is 2P No. 568, waiting to assist over the Mendips to Bath, the 10.16 a.m. (SO) Bournemouth to Nottingham and Cleethorpes. *16th September, 1950*

41. Let battle commence! 2P No. 568 and 'Black Five' No. 44945 make a typically vigorous departure northwards from Evercreech Junction. The train was the 9.25 a.m. (SO) Bournemouth to Manchester and Liverpool, and facing them immediately was the 8½ mile climb, much of it at 1 in 50, up to Masbury Summit. 811 feet above sea level. *12th August, 1950*

**BATH, GREEN PARK
—ARRIVALS**

42. 'Black Five' No. 44825—immaculate in experimental light green livery, and with **BRITISH RAILWAYS** on the tender—runs in past the turntable queue, with the 7.33 a.m. (SO) Nottingham to Bournemouth.
19th August, 1950

43. With the driver of the leading engine judging nicely the final cautious approach to the terminus buffer stops, 2P No. 40564 and 4F No. 44557 arrive with a Saturday relief from Bournemouth to the North. In the middle distance, a 'Jinty' tank stands coupled to a gas container wagon, ready to top up the gas supply for the dining car cookers.
19th August, 1950

44. On August Bank Holiday Monday, 4F No. 44417, in charge of the 3.10 p.m. down local to Templecombe, sets off past sister engine No. 44523, standing outside the Midland shed.

7th August, 1950

45. A Caprotti 'Black Five', No. 44744, setting off north from Bath with the 9.25 a.m. (SO) Bournemouth to Manchester and Liverpool.

19th August, 1950

A Caprotti '5' had not yet been tried out over the S & D, but the date of the first run was not far distant—1951 was to see the first run of one of these engines over the line.

THE S.R. PACIFIC TRIALS OVER THE S & D

46. 'Battle of Britain' Pacific No. 34109 "Sir Trafford Leigh Mallory" comes in over Bath Junction on Wednesday, 14th March, with the 11.40 a.m. from Bournemouth up to Bath. This was the first test of the series and was really a 'familiarisation' run, for the load was only four coaches—a mere featherweight as far as the Pacific was concerned.

14th March, 1951

47. The arrival of No. 34109 on Bath shed caused great interest amongst the staff, for the engine bristled with unorthodox features and advanced thinking in steam locomotive design. Standing beside No. 34109 are (left) foreman fitter George Adams, and driver Donald Beale who had brought the engine up from Bournemouth.

14th March, 1951

1951

With the Southern Region responsible for motive power on the Somerset & Dorset—but, in fact, providing none of the locomotives, all of which were still on loan from the London Midland Region—the motive power situation was rather incongruous.

So it was really no surprise when news broke that the Southern Region were making arrangements to carry out a series of test runs over the Somerset & Dorset with one of their Bulleid Light Pacifics. This most interesting event was undoubtedly the S & D 'highlight' of the year. The trials took place in March, and the locomotive used was No. 34109 "Sir Trafford Leigh Mallory", one of the latest in the 'Battle of Britain' class, and at the time, less than one year old, having entered service in May 1950.

Following these trials, four Bulleid Light Pacifics were allocated to Bath motive power depot.

48. Prior to the run up from Bournemouth the Southern authorities had checked that Bath had a 60 ft. turntable and therefore the engine could be turned. But when it actually came to turning No. 34109, it was found that positioning the engine, with her wheelbase of 57 ft. 6 in., on Bath's 60 ft. turntable, called for infinite care and precision. The overall length of a Bulleid Light Pacific was 67 ft. 4¾ in., so there was a considerable overhang, and if the engine was positioned just a shade too far forward, then, as the turning proceeded, the leading buffers would foul wagons standing on the coal stage road.

14th March, 1951

49. The close proximity to the turntable of loaded wagons standing on the coal stage road *did* have advantages for some! By astute positioning of their engine on the table, the crew of 2-6-2T No. 41242, finding themselves rather low on fuel, were able to practise a little 'self-help'!

50.

No. 34109's return run home in the afternoon was with the 4.25 p.m. down semi-fast from Bath to Bournemouth (3.25 p.m. ex Gloucester). Since the up run, there had been a steady deterioration in the weather, and by the time the train left Bath, it was raining. In this picture No. 34109—with her electric lights shining brightly—is emerging from Chilcompton Tunnel into the growing gloom of a wet March afternoon.

14th March, 1951

51. As the trials proceeded, the load was increased steadily. The climax came on Wednesday, 21st March, when No. 34109 was rostered to haul the up "Pines Express", loaded to ten coaches with no assistance being given for the climb over the Mendips from Evercreech Junction to Bath. This proved to be beyond the engine's capability, and with speed down to little more than walking pace at Masbury Summit, Bath was eventually reached some ten minutes late. This picture shows the train running in past the entrance to Bath Sheds. The weather on this day was very dull and overcast, but fortunately dry. Had it not been, Nemesis would undoubtedly have struck!

21st March, 1951

52. During some of the early runs over the S & D by Southern Pacifics, there were one or two 'misses' with the tablet exchange apparatus, but this initial trouble was quickly sorted out. In this picture, taken from the footplate of No. 34037 "Clovelly", Mr. Elliott, the Bath shedmaster, is personally checking the setting of the catcher with the device specially constructed for this purpose.

25th May, 1951

53. 'Battle of Britain' Pacific No. 34109 "Sir Trafford Leigh Mallory"—the engine used for all the trial runs over the S & D—poses on Bath turntable. Note that by this date, 24th March, a tablet catcher bracket had been fitted to her tender. It will also be seen that both discs covering access to the sandboxes are open. They may have been opened to check the sand contents, but it is more likely that they had vibrated open during the run up from Bournemouth. As a result of this trait, which allowed rain to run into the sandboxes—and also other difficulties encountered in replenishing the sandboxes—No. 34109, and those of her sister engines with the same circular 'surface' fillers, were modified to the standard recessed square sandbox fillers.

24th March, 1951

54. Having learnt the lesson the hard way on 21st March, when No. 34109 had only just escaped stalling whilst trying to take ten coaches over Masbury Summit unaided, the maximum load laid down for the Bulleid Light Pacifics was fixed at 270 tons (eight coaches) the same for the Stanier 'Black Fives'. So when on Saturday, 24th March, No. 34109 was rostered to haul the down "Pines Express", she was given an assisting engine, 2P 4-4-0 No. 40563, for the run from Bath over the Mendips down to Evercreech Junction. In this picture they are climbing towards Chilcompton rock cutting. Inspector Hookey, who rode on No. 34109 throughout the trials, may just be discerned leaning out of the Pacific's cab.

24th March, 1951

Following the trials in March of S.R. Pacific No. 34109, four of the class were allocated to Bath M.P.D. They were:—
No. 34040 "Crewkerne".
No. 34041 "Wilton".
No. 34042 "Dorchester".
No. 34043 "Combe Martin".

55. The up "Pines Express" hauled by 2P No. 40564 and S.R. Pacific No. 34040 "Crewkerne", coming up through the rock cutting towards Masbury Summit on a lovely summer's day in August. The 8½ mile climb from Evercreech Junction had certainly not 'winded' the 2P, which started to blow off furiously as she neared the summit!

18th August, 1951

56. 3F 0-6-0 No. 43204—built for the S & D J R in 1896—and S.R. Pacific No. 34041 "Wilton" draw to a stand at Binegar with an up relief express on the last Saturday in July. Traffic over the S & D on this day was very heavy and all available motive power was stretched to the limit. Normal procedure for up expresses requiring assistance over the Mendips was for the pilot engine to work through from Evercreech Junction to Bath. On this Saturday however, pilots of some up relief trains, including this one, were coming off at Binegar, leaving the train engine to carry on to Bath on her own. Meanwhile the pilot engine was hurrying back, tender-first, light engine, to Evercreech Junction to assist another train up the southern slopes of the Mendips.

The main snag to this working was that it left Bath short of pilots for any extra southbound trains later in the day.

28th July, 1951

57. 4F 0-6-0 No. 44558—built for the S & D J R in 1922—and S.R. Pacific No. 34042 "Dorchester", in charge of the 9.55 a.m. (SO) Bournemouth to Leeds, negotiate the sharp curve just north of Evercreech Junction, and start the long and arduous 8½ mile climb up to Masbury Summit.

21st July, 1951

58. The fourth of Bath's Southern Pacifics, No. 34043 "Combe Martin", climbing away from Radstock with a down stopping train. The line in the foreground is the ex-Great Western North Somerset line, over the top of which the S & D train is about to pass.

4th August, 1951

59. 2P No. 40568 and 'West Country' Pacific No. 34093 "Saunton" climbing towards Chilcompton Tunnel with the down "Pines" relief. No. 40568 had only just come back from Derby after a general overhaul, and was immaculate in lined-out black livery.

16th June, 1951

PACIFICS FROM BOURNEMOUTH CENTRAL SHED WORKING OVER THE SOMERSET AND DORSET

Even with the allocation of four S.R. Pacifics to Bath M.P.D., the Somerset and Dorset had not got enough motive power to haul the many additional trains which ran over the line on summer Saturdays between the Midlands and North of England, and Bournemouth. To help cope with this situation, Bournemouth Central shed provided several Bulleid Light Pacifics for summer Saturday use over the S & D.

60. On a warm summer's evening in early June, 'West Country' No. 34037 "Clovelly", breasts Masbury Summit with the 3.35 p.m. from Bournemouth—the 'Up Mail'.

5th June, 1951

61. The 7.33 a.m. (SO) Nottingham to Bournemouth setting off from Bath hauled by 2P No. 40697 and 'West Country' No. 34044 "Woolacombe" and (62, right) as they pass by, a close-up of the Pacific's cheerful crew, driver Arthur Clist and fireman Edward Skinner.

14th July, 1951

—AND AN INTERESTING 'RARE BIRD' ON THE S & D

63. 2P No. 40601—working really hard—and Caprotti 'Black Five' No. 44754 climbing up through Horsecombe Vale towards Combe Down Tunnel with the 2.45 p.m. (SO) Bournemouth to Bristol. This is thought to have been one of the first runs over the S & D by a Caprotti 'Black Five'. (She had worked an express down to Bournemouth in the morning.) The following Saturday I saw the Caprotti's driver on Bath shed, and asked him how the engine had performed. 'Oh', he said, 'She went like the wind downhill, but wouldn't pull the skin off a rice pudding up the banks!'

4th August, 1951

THE OTHER END OF THE MOTIVE POWER SCALE—THE S & D's TWO EX-MIDLAND RAILWAY 2Ps

In 1951 the Somerset and Dorset had a stud of twelve 2P 4-4-0s. Two of these engines, Nos. 40505 and 40509, were real 'old ladies', having been built for the Midland Railway in 1899 by Sharp Stewart and Co. In 1912 509 (her M.R. number) was extensively rebuilt at Derby with a larger boiler, Belpaire firebox, superheater and 20½ in. x 26 in. cylinders. 505 was similarly rebuilt sometime prior to 1920.

These ex-Midland 2Ps differed from the later L.M.S. type 2Ps in having larger coupled wheels of 7 ft. 0½ in. diameter, and right hand drive. Both 40505 and 40509 were shedded at Templecombe.

65. On a lovely spring afternoon in late April, 2P No. 40505 leaves Midford viaduct with the 4.37 p.m. down stopping train from Bath to Templecombe.

21st April, 1951

64. Ex-M.R. 2P 4-4-0 No. 40505 standing in Bath, Green Park, Station on a dull afternoon in early April. By 1951 No. 40505 had acquired a tall Stanier chimney, which marred slightly her graceful appearance.

7th April, 1951

66. No. 40509 at Binegar on a sunny Tuesday evening in April. With driver Gibbons in charge, 40509 is in the process of running round her train, the 6.05 p.m. (SX) local from Bath to Binegar. The return working was the 7.10 p.m. (SX) Binegar to Bath, which 40509 would have to take back to Bath, tender first—quite pleasant for the crew on a sunny spring evening like this, but very different if it had been wet! (This was normally a tank engine working.) *24th April, 1951*

67. No. 40509 climbing uphill over Prestleigh viaduct with the 4.15 p.m. Templecombe —Bath stopping train. *28th April, 1951*

68. For many years it had been almost an institution for a Templecombe 2P to pilot the up "Pines Express" from Evercreech Junction over the Mendips to Bath in the morning, returning with the down train in the afternoon. Although the two ex-Midland 2Ps were a lot older than Templecombe's ex-L.M.S. standard 2Ps, there was never any hesitation in 1951 in using 40505 and 40509, turn and turn about, with the other 2Ps for this job.

In this picture 2P No. 40509 and S.R. Pacific No. 34041 "Wilton" are swinging through the reverse curves south of Midford with the down "Pines Express". *21st July, 1951*

THE S & D 7F 2-8-0s AT WORK

69. With a towering column of exhaust indicating how hard she was working, 7F No. 53800 comes thundering up the 1 in 50 bank out of Bath with the 12.35 p.m. down freight to Evercreech Junction. Hearty assistance was being given in the rear by a 4F 0-6-0, which would drop off at the end of the climb, just before the entrance to Combe Down Tunnel.

28th April, 1951

70. After taking the 12.35 p.m. freight from Bath down to Evercreech Junction (see picture 69 opposite), 7F No. 53800 returned to Bath with the 5.15 p.m. up freight from Evercreech Junction. She is seen here in the early evening, coasting downhill with her train towards Moorewood.

28th April, 1951

71. On a fine spring afternoon in late April, 7F No. 53809 drops downhill past Midford goods yard with the 3.48 p.m. goods from Bath. (Always referred to by S & D staff as "The Market"—see picture 34.)

21st April, 1951

72. S & D 7F 2-8-0 No. 53807 standing on Bath shed.

21st April, 1951

S & D 7F 2-8-0 No. 53807

In 1951 there were three of the 1925 series S & D 7Fs still retaining a large boiler. One of these was No. 53807.

73. The maker's plate of 7F No. 53807.

74. Although it is jumping ahead of our period, this later view of No. 53807 makes an interesting comparison with the picture of her above for it shows how the engine looked after she had been rebuilt in 1954 with one of the smaller boilers of 4 ft 9$\frac{1}{8}$ in. diameter.

7Fs ON PASSENGER WORK

As in 1950, occasional, reluctant use had to be made of the 7Fs for hauling passenger trains, but this practice was kept to an absolute minimum, and only used as a last resort.

75. On a hot and oppressive Saturday in late July, 2P No. 40564 and 7F No. 53805 toil up the last few yards to Masbury Summit with a heavy, twelve coach relief train from Nottingham to Bournemouth.

28th July, 1951

—AND A 7F TO THE RESCUE!

76. The up "Pines Express" climbing past Masbury Halt, hauled by Stanier 'Black Five' No. 44830, and piloted by large-boilered 7F 2-8-0 No. 53806. This very rare sight came about due to the "Pines" normal pilot—a 2P 4-4-0—being commandeered at short notice to take over a down train, when the Bulleid Pacific hauling it, failed at Evercreech Junction. When the up "Pines Express" rolled into the Junction, the only engine available to assist the 'Black Five' in the climb over the Mendips was No. 53806. I was told later that as the train was only one coach over the limit for a class '5', the 7F came off at Binegar, and 44830 then took the "Pines" on to Bath on her own. Had it not been such a stormy day, it is more than likely that the driver of 44830 would also have been prepared to 'have a go' at taking the nine coaches up to Masbury Summit on his own.

3rd November, 1951

TWO OF A KIND
IN DOUBLE-HARNESS

The S & D was renowned for producing interesting combinations of locomotives on double-headed trains. Here are two examples of sister engines working together.

77. A lovely May morning, a dry rail, and an abundance of power—the up "Pines" relief sails up the 1 in 50 through the rock cutting towards Masbury Summit, hauled by two Stanier 'Black Fives', Nos. 45440 and 44839. 45440 was one of the S & D's first 'Black Fives', having come to the line (as 5440) in 1938 when just a few months old.

12th May, 1951

78. Two 4F 0-6-0s, Nos. 44146 and 44557, burst out of Combe Down Tunnel with the 10.38 a.m. (SO) Manchester to Bournemouth. No. 44146 was an ex-L.M.S. Crewe-built engine, whilst No. 44557 was built for the S & D J R in 1922 by Armstrong Whitworth & Co.

4th August, 1951

79. 2P No. 40698 gets under way with the 5.50 p.m. Bristol–Bournemouth (7.00 p.m. off Bath), whilst in the far platform 2-6-2T No. 41243 prepares to leave at 7.05 p.m. for the run up to Mangotsfield with the 'Up Mail' (3.35 p.m. off Bournemouth).

25th May, 1951

EVENING
AT
BATH, GREEN PARK

80. 'West Country' Pacific No. 34043 "Combe Martin" basks in the evening sunshine during a short pause in her carriage shunting duties.

2nd June, 1951

81. The sight that never ceased to entrance me—the line-up of pilot engines in the centre road on a summer Saturday morning, waiting to assist up expresses over the Mendips. On this occasion the engines were—4F 0-6-0 No. 44535 and 2P 4-4-0s Nos. 40564, 40697 and 40568.

18th August, 1951

EVERCREECH JUNCTION

82. Johnson 1P 0-4-4 tank No. 58046 sets off briskly from Evercreech Junction with a stopping train for Templecombe.
21st July, 1951

83. 2P No. 40568 and 'Black Five' No. 44839 departing in very determined style for the 8½ mile climb up to Masbury Summit with the 9.25 a.m. (SO) Bournemouth to Manchester and Liverpool. The driver of the 2P is Clifford West, whilst Bert Brewer is in charge of the class '5'.

21st July, 1951

84. Johnson 3F 0-6-0 No. 43419 draws into Evercreech Junction down yard in the early afternoon with a lengthy goods off the branch.

21st July, 1951

JOHNSON ENGINES ON THE S & D

In 1951, two types of locomotives designed by S.W. Johnson for the Midland Railway towards the end of the last century, were still giving solid, reliable service on the S & D—the 1P 0-4-4 tank (left, picture 82) and the 3F 0-6-0 (right, picture 84).

BATH MOTIVE POWER DEPOT

85. Standing outside the S & D shed on a sunny April morning—2P No. 40697, 4F No. 44561 and—being coaled—2P No. 40696.

21st April, 1951

86. A summer Saturday line-up of three Stanier 'Black Fives' (the leading one a Caprotti) waiting to take over expresses for the Midlands and the North of England, after their arrival from Bournemouth. The engines are Nos. 44757, 44849 and 44842.

14th July, 1951

HIGHBRIDGE MOTIVE POWER DEPOT

87. Two generations of tank-engines standing side by side on Highbridge shed—0-4-4T No. 58047 designed by S.W. Johnson in 1881, and 2-6-2T No. 41241, an H.G. Ivatt design of 1946. The 2-6-2T was on loan from Bath shed. No. 58047 was the last Johnson tank on the S & D to retain Salter valves on the dome, and a round topped firebox.

12th August, 1951

88. Two Johnson tanks, Nos. 58086 and 58088, standing outside the east end of Highbridge shed. Both engines had been rebuilt with Belpaire fireboxes and closed domes.

5th August, 1951

89. On the last Saturday in July, so many extra trains were being run from the Midlands and the North down to Bournemouth, that the S & D must have come close to saturation point! In the early morning driver Epps, with 7F No. 53805, had taken a ten-coach Birmingham relief from Bath down to Bournemouth, but with no return working it meant coming back home, light engine—no doubt a rather tedious and protracted journey. Approaching Cole in the late afternoon, driver Epps found the Up Home signal against him, and is seen here about to bring 53805 to a stand. They were close on the heels of a heavy northbound relief, which was probably exceeding her allotted time at Evercreech Junction for taking water and attaching a pilot engine for the climb over the Mendips.
26th July, 1952

1952

'7Fs WITH EVERYTHING!'

The year started quite normally but, for railway enthusiasts, exciting things were to happen before the summer was out. In the late spring Mr. Arthur Elliott, the Bath shedmaster—or shed foreman as the appointment was known in those days—retired. Mr. Elliott, a life-long locomotive man—and, incidentally, a very strict disciplinarian—had never been keen on the use of the S & D 7F 2-8-0s on passenger trains. However, as we have seen, at the height of the summer service in 1950 and 1951, intense weekend traffic had left him with no alternative but to use the 7Fs, albeit with great reluctance and some foreboding.

Mr. Webb, the new shedmaster, had no such scruples, and during the 1952 summer service, wide use was made of the 7Fs for passenger work, both as train engines and as pilots. This new move did not please many of the footplatemen, for whereas the 7Fs, with their eight 4 ft. 8½ in. coupled wheels, may have been excellent engines for hauling heavy trains *up* the Mendips, they gave one a jolly rough ride when running helter-skelter down the other side!

90. After bringing in the up "Pines", it was found that class '5' No. 44917 was running hot. The Bath shedmaster, Mr. Derek Webb (second from right), discusses the trouble with drivers Bert Brewer, Harold Barber, and fireman 'Bill' Bailey.

AN UNEVENTFUL START
TO THE YEAR

91. Bath, Green Park, station on a fine afternoon in early March. Ivatt 2-6-2T No. 41240 is about to set off with a local train for Bristol, whilst sister engine No. 41243 draws out from the right hand platform after bringing in the 3.30 p.m. Bristol—Bournemouth semi-fast (which had just departed behind a class 2P 4-4-0). Standing in the middle road, waiting for the platform to become free, is ex-Midland 2P 4-4-0 No. 40505 with the stock for the 4.37 p.m. down stopping train for Temple-combe.

8th March, 1952

92. 2P 4-4-0 No. 40563 and Bulleid Pacific No. 34044 "Woolacombe" drifting in over Bath Junction with the up "Pines Express". Although not an S & D engine, "Woolacombe" was often to be seen working over the line, for she appeared to be Bournemouth M.P.D.'s 'first choice' when asked to provide one of their Pacifics for a turn over the S & D up to Bath and back.

17th May, 1952

THE CALM BEFORE THE EXCITEMENT

Normal power for the "Pines Express", and other through trains to and from the North, was either a Bulleid Pacific or a Stanier 'Black Five', with a 2P 4-4-0 assisting over the Mendips if the load exceeded 270 tons (eight coaches).

93. 2P No. 40563 and Bulleid Pacific No. 34042 "Dorchester" emerge from Devonshire Tunnel into the fresh air of Lyncombe Vale with the down "Pines Express". Smoke and fumes can be seen pouring from the ¼ mile long, unventilated and very restricted bore of Devonshire Tunnel through which the line climbed at 1 in 50. The clearance between the top of a Bulleid Pacific and the roof of the tunnel was less than one foot, and during the passage up through the tunnel, conditions on the footplate of the second engine of a double-headed train could be really dreadful—no wonder S & D footplatemen often referred to Devonshire Tunnel as 'Dante's Inferno'!

3rd June, 1952

94. 2P No. 40700 and Stanier 'Black Five' No. 44830, making light work of the climb out of Bath, come charging up the 1 in 50 towards Devonshire Tunnel with a Whit Sunday excursion from Bristol to Bournemouth. In 1952, apart from excursion traffic, there was just one scheduled Sunday passenger train over the S & D, and then only from 6th July to 14th September. This was the 9.30 a.m. Bristol—Bournemouth (10.08 a.m. off Bath) and the return working, which left Bournemouth at 7.05 p.m.

1st June, 1952

95.

Quite early in the season there were signs that the summer of 1952 was going to be a pretty hectic time for the Somerset and Dorset. By late July virtually every engine that could turn a wheel, was pressed into service on Saturdays—not to mention any 'foreign' engine that could be surreptitiously 'borrowed' for the weekend!

This Birmingham—Bournemouth relief, seen passing through Cole, was composed of ex-L.N.E.R. stock and hauled by a 'borrowed' 'Black Five', No. 45059 from Saltley.

26th July, 1952

96.

One of the typical summer Saturday scenes at Bath—engines 'queueing up' for the turntable. Two 'Black Fives', which have been turned, are setting back so as to allow 2P No. 40563 and S.R. Pacific No. 34042 "Dorchester" to run up to the turntable.

21st June, 1952

97. Traffic on the first Saturday in August was so heavy that some up trains, after passing over Masbury Summit, detached their pilots at Binegar, so that they could hurry back down to Evercreech Junction to assist another train up the southern slopes of the Mendips. This up express, preparing to come to a stand at Binegar, had a delightful locomotive combination. The train engine was a modern Bulleid Pacific, No. 34040 "Crewkerne", whilst the pilot was an elderly Johnson 3F 0-6-0, No. 43204, built for the S & D J R in 1896—50 years before the Pacific!

2nd August, 1952

THE SOMERSET AND DORSET 7Fs
—ON THEIR NORMAL WORK

98. On a bright winter's afternoon in late February, No. 53803—one of the original 1914 series—shunts Shepton Mallet yard before proceeding on her way with the 1.45 p.m. up goods from Evercreech Junction to Midsomer Norton.

23rd February, 1952

99.

No. 53810—one of the re-boilered 1925 series—prepares to set off from Bath with the 3.48 p.m. down pick-up goods to Evercreech Junction. Coupled next to the engine is one of the Sentinel four-wheeled shunters, No. 47190, which had just come back from overhaul, and was being returned to Radstock.

8th March, 1952

101. Driver Horace Clarke looks out happily from the cab as No. 53807, obviously steaming well, climbs southwards from Binegar towards Masbury Summit with a down coal train. Giving hearty banking assistance in the rear is 0-6-0T No. 47557.

15th March, 1952

100. No. 53806, in the charge of driver Fred Holmes, climbing away from Radstock with the 12.35 p.m. down goods from Bath to Evercreech Junction.

8th March, 1952

THE SOMERSET AND DORSET 7F 2-8-0s ON PASSENGER TRAINS— HANDLING UP TO TEN COACHES, UNASSISTED OVER THE MENDIPS

102. No. 53800, the doyen of the class, standing in Evercreech Junction station after bringing in a heavy 12-coach relief from Bournemouth to the North. Ron Bryant, the 7F's fireman, has just removed the reporting number from the front of the 7F for transfer to the 2P which was to pilot them over the Mendips to Bath.

12th July, 1952

103. On a wet and dismal Saturday in early August, No. 53804 coasts in over the level crossing at the southern end of Evercreech Junction station, with a relief from Bournemouth to Manchester.

9th August, 1952

104. No. 53809, the preserved 7F which is kept at The Midland Railway Trust at Butterley, running swiftly downhill towards Evercreech Junction with a relief from Walsall to Bournemouth. Shortly before taking this picture, I had had a nasty moment! A large black car suddenly appeared on the private road leading to a farm, and stopped. My immediate, guilty reaction was that I had been caught, redhanded, by the farmer, standing in the middle of his hayfield! But to my great relief, the car driver turned out to be my friend Patrick Whitehouse, down from Birmingham on an 'S & D Safari'.

26th July, 1952

105. After running up the spur (seen left) to call at Templecombe Upper, and then having been drawn out backwards to Templecombe No. 2 Junction, large-boilered 7F No. 53807 resumes her journey to Bournemouth with the 7.33 a.m. (SO) from Nottingham. The last 32 miles from Midford down to Templecombe had been double track, but 53807 now had 16 miles of single line to traverse as far as Blandford Forum.

26th July, 1952

S & D 7Fs ON PASSENGER TRAINS —WITH PILOT ASSISTANCE

106. 2P No. 40698 and 7F No. 53804 standing in Shepton Mallet station with the 7.43 a.m. (SO) Birmingham to Bournemouth, where there was a booked stop of five minutes for taking water. This train then ran non-stop to Wincanton, so having the distinction of being the only express not scheduled to call at Evercreech Junction.

19th July, 1952

107. Five weeks later, the 7.43 a.m. (SO) Birmingham to Bournemouth was again hauled by 7F No. 53804, but this time she had a 4F 0-6-0, No. 44096, as pilot. Nearing Binegar, the train was running some five minutes late, and as can be seen from their near-vertical exhausts, both engines were being worked very hard in an endeavour to regain time.

23rd August, 1952

108. 2P No. 40696 and 7F No. 53809 dropping down past the grounds of Midford Castle with the 8.20 a.m. (SO) Bristol to Bournemouth.

12th July, 1952

109. 2P No. 40696 and 7F No. 53802 running fast downhill towards Prestleigh with a relief from the Midlands.

2nd August, 1952

110. Our friend the 7.43 a.m. (SO) Birmingham to Bournemouth again, this time hauled by 2P No. 40700 and 7F No. 53810, draws near to Evercreech Junction. At the height of the summer service, trains from the Midlands and the North sometimes produced a most interesting variety of unusual coaching stock. On this express, the coach next to the 7F is an ex-Great Central Railway 'Barnum' brake end saloon of 1911 vintage.

26th July, 1952

111. 7F No. 53809 and Bulleid 'West Country' Pacific No. 34042 "Dorchester" round the sharp curve just north of Evercreech Junction with the 9.55 a.m. (SO) Bournemouth to Leeds. Ahead of them now lay the 8½ mile climb—much of it at 1 in 50—over the Mendips. The day was stormy, with sudden squalls of rain, and no doubt the Pacific's driver was glad to have such a powerful and sure-footed pilot for the climb up to Masbury Summit.

9th August, 1952

THE SOMERSET AND DORSET 7F 2-8-0s
AS ASSISTING ENGINES ON PASSENGER TRAINS

No. 53809 is the 7F which has been preserved by Mr. Frank Beaumont and is now 'in residence' at Butterley, the headquarters of The Midland Railway Trust in Derbyshire.

112. An hour after taking the picture on the left, another 7F appeared on pilot duty. This time it was No. 53810 assisting a fellow ex-S & D engine, 4F No. 44559, with a nine coach relief from Bournemouth to the North. As the engines climbed steadily up the 1 in 50 towards Prestleigh, the wind, which had now increased to near gale force, snatched savagely at their exhaust and sent it streaming away eastwards over the open hillside.

9th August, 1952

113. On a fine evening in mid July, 7F No. 53808 and Stanier 'Black Five' No. 45440, came sweeping through the reverse curves towards Wellow with the 2.45 p.m. (SO) Bournemouth to Bristol.

19th July, 1952

No. 53808 is the 7F owned by the Somerset and Dorset Railway Museum Trust, and is being restored to running order at the Trust's headquarters at Washford, on the West Somerset railway. In 1952 53808 still had a large boiler, but this was replaced by one of the smaller type G9AS boilers in 1953, and this is the form in which the engine is now preserved.

**AND THE ULTIMATE!
—TWO S & D 7F 2-8-0s
IN 'DOUBLE-HARNESS' ON
A PASSENGER TRAIN**

114. A very rare sight—something I only saw six times in forty years—two S & D 7Fs in double-harness on a passenger train. On this occasion the train was the 6.05 a.m. Bristol to Bournemouth (6.55 a.m. off Bath) and the locomotive combination was particularly fascinating as both types of S & D 7F were represented. The leading 7F, No. 53807, is one of the large-boilered 1925 series, whilst the train engine is No. 53800, the first of the 1914 series. The pair are seen here, running down past the grounds of Midford Castle with their train which was composed of only six bogies, and so could have been handled with the greatest of ease by one 7F on her own. The reason for the second 7F was that she was being worked down to Bournemouth in order to bring an unbalanced relief up to Bath later in the day.

12th July, 1952

115. After photographing the train nearing Midford, I drove rapidly over to Radstock for a second shot, and then got this final picture of the two 7Fs just setting off from their Binegar stop.

12th July, 1952

Whereas on summer Saturdays in 1952, the limelight may have been on the 7F 2-8-0s in use on passenger trains, during these days of intense traffic, all S & D engines gave outstanding service—and none more so than the stud of 4F 0-6-0s.

116. Two 4F 0-6-0s, Nos. 44146 and 44559 running in over Bath Junction with the 10.40 a.m. (SO) Bournemouth to Manchester. (According to the W.T.T., the previous Saturday should have been its last run in 1952!) On the right, 7F No. 53804 is drifting back onto a down goods train which she will take out as soon as the single line to Midford becomes clear.

20th September, 1952

117. 2P No. 40563 and 4F No. 44561 passing over Tucking Mill viaduct in charge of the 6.52 a.m. (SO) Cleethorpes to Bournemouth. (In later years the destination of this train was changed to Exmouth.) Note that Tucking Mill viaduct had been widened to take double track, but the second line was never laid.

19th July, 1952

EVERCREECH JUNCTION

As usual, offering superb entertainment for the railway enthusiast on a summer Saturday.

118. Mr. O.S. Nock, the eminent railway author, draws his wife's attention to the line-up of assisting engines standing in the middle road.

5th July, 1952

119. One of the fascinations of Evercreech Junction on a summer Saturday was to watch the assisting engines arriving and assembling in the middle road. Some would come up from Templecombe, light engine, whilst others, which had assisted down trains over the Mendips earlier in the morning, would be turned on the table by the North Box, and then come backing down into the station. Shortly before the first of the procession of up expresses was due, four—and at the height of the season, five—assisting engines would be ready, waiting buffer to buffer, lined up in the middle road. On this first Saturday in July, the line-up—starting with the leading engine—consisted of 4F No. 44123, 2P No. 40564, 4F No. 44417 and 4F No. 44559. The trains they were to assist were—9.25 a.m. Manchester and Liverpool, 9.45 a.m. Manchester, 9.55 a.m. Leeds and 10.05 a.m. Nottingham (all 'Saturdays only' ex Bournemouth West).

5th July, 1952

120. Punctually at 10.47 'Black Five' No. 44830 rolled in with the 9.25 from Bournemouth. As soon as she had come to a stand, the station foreman gave the bell code to the signalman, points were changed, and 4F No. 44123 moved smartly out onto the main line and then set back carefully onto 44830. Then, in what seemed no time at all, and with both engines blowing off vigorously, they were away—and the 8½ mile 'battle' up to Masbury Summit was on.

5th July, 1952

121. My son Julian and a girlfriend gaze out happily from the cab of Johnson 0-4-4T No. 58051 after being invited to climb aboard by driver Charlie King. 58051 and her two coaches were stabled in the middle road prior to forming the 4.48 p.m. branch line train to Highbridge.

30th August, 1952

122.

2P No. 40564 and S.R. Pacific No. 34043 "Combe Martin", with her newly modified tender, get away smoothly with the 9.45 a.m. (SO) Bournemouth to Manchester.

5th July, 1952

123.

The up "Pines" arrives at Evercreech Junction hauled by 'West Country' Pacific No. 34043 "Combe Martin" carrying a new Southern-type headboard for this celebrated express. Unfortunately it was not found possible to fix the new headboard to the front of the ex-L.M.S. 2P pilot engine which came on at Evercreech Junction to assist over the Mendips to Bath. So for the 26 miles between Evercreech Junction and Bath the headboard could not be carried by the leading engine, and sadly as a result this soon led to "The Pines Express" headboard quietly vanishing from the scene.
27th June, 1953

(A Western Region style headboard—from which they omitted the word 'THE'—did appear briefly in 1962 for the final days that this famous express ran over the Somerset and Dorset.)

1953

Apart from Bath's turntable disgracing itself, and the brief appearance of a headboard for "The Pines Express", 1953, by S & D standards, was quite a normal year. Traffic remained good—and even hectic on Saturdays at the height of the summer service.

For some time, the London Midland Region had been pressing for the return of their Stanier 'Black Fives', still on loan to the Southern Region, and in October, when the summer service had come to an end, three of these engines, Nos. 44826, 44830 and 44839 were returned to the London Midland Region. This left the S & D with just two 'Black Fives', Nos. 44917 and the 'old faithful', 45440. Speculation was rife as to what would replace the 'Black Fives' next year, one rumour being that the S & D was to get some of the B.R. 'Clan' class Pacifics. For what did actually happen, see 1954!

The pictures for 1953 take us down the line as far as Evercreech Junction.

124. The late Arthur Polden, day foreman at Bath Green Park shed. Arthur was a very good friend of mine, and many of my most interesting pictures were taken as a direct result of his kindness in passing on to me information about special trains, unusual locomotive workings, etc.

25th May, 1953

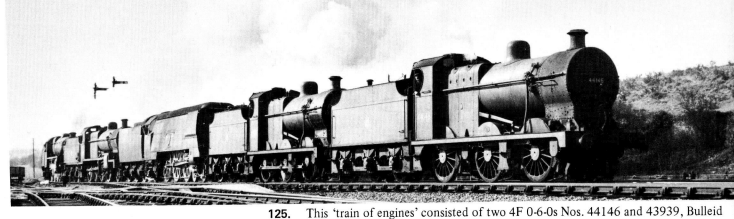

125. This 'train of engines' consisted of two 4F 0-6-0s Nos. 44146 and 43939, Bulleid Pacific No. 34042 "Dorchester", S & D 7F 2-8-0 No. 53805 and Stanier 'Black Five' 4-6-0 No. 44848. After arriving from Bath, tender first, the five engines are seen here at Mangotsfield setting off forwards up the Bristol—Gloucester main line, for the short run to the North Junction.

7th April, 1953

BATH'S TURNTABLE OUT OF ACTION

Only a little over two years after being renovated, the turntable at Bath developed mechanical trouble and had to be taken out of service for a week. Whilst repairs were being carried out, the only way S & D engines could be turned, was by running them ten miles up the Midland line to the triangle junction at Mangotsfield. To lessen the operating problems involved, engines were assembled in groups of four or five, and then run, coupled together as a 'train of engines', up to Mangotsfield and back. Special paths were arranged for these workings and on average, one hour was allowed for the round trip.

126. The S & D engines passing through Mangotsfield station on their way up to the North Junction.

7th April, 1953

127. —and coming back, now running tender first, past the South Junction at the start of their run back to Bath.

7th April, 1953

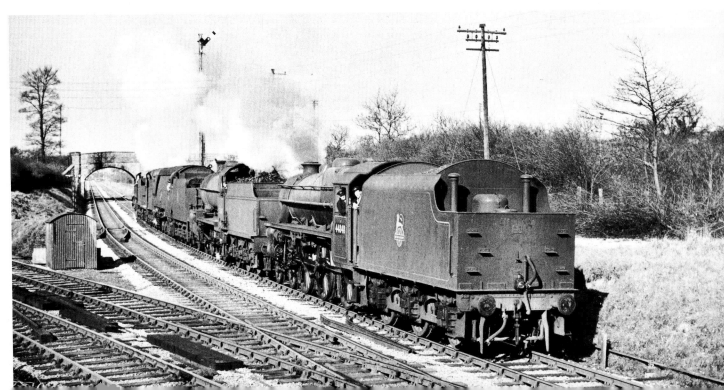

BATH JUNCTION

128. The load over the Mendips for a Stanier 'Black Five' or a Bulleid Pacific was 270 tons (8 coaches). However, if the necessity arose, many S & D footplate crews would be prepared to take 'one over the eight' over the Mendips without a pilot—if their engine was a 'Black Five' in good condition, and the weather was fine. On the second Saturday in June, the 9.55 a.m. (SO) Bournemouth to Leeds was made up to nine, and for some reason, there was no pilot engine available at Evercreech Junction. So the crew of Stanier 'Black Five' No. 44839 had brought the train up from Evercreech Junction on their own, and are seen here passing over Bath Junction, 'right time'.

13th June, 1953

129. Four weeks later, No. 44839 had the same train again. This time, however, the load was twelve bogies, and for the climb over the Mendips she had the assistance of an old S & D stalwart—3F 0-6-0 No. 43194, originally No. 62, which had been built for the S & D J R at Derby in 1896.

11th July, 1953

DEVONSHIRE TUNNEL

130. 2P No. 40601 and large-boilered 7F No. 53808 climb up the 1 in 50 out of Devonshire Tunnel and into Lyncombe Vale with the 7.35 a.m. (SO) Nottingham to Bournemouth.

4th July, 1953

With the arrival of summer, passenger traffic over the S & D on Saturdays began to increase rapidly, and very early in the season, Bath shed found themselves having to resort to the use of the 7F 2-8-0s, in addition to 'borrowing' any suitable 'foreign' engines that might just happen to be available.

131. 'Snowploughs in June!' 'Borrowed' 'Black Five' No. 44883 coasts out of Devonshire Tunnel with the 3.35 p.m. up from Bournemouth. Although the shed staff at Bath were past masters at 'borrowing' 'foreign' engines, they must surely have surpassed themselves on this occasion, for 'Black Five' No. 44883 was a Scottish Region engine from 68A, Carlisle (Kingmoor) shed! (I wonder what the Carlisle shedmaster would have said, had he known his engine had been as far south as Bournemouth!)

6th June, 1953

THE MIDFORD VALLEY

132. Saturday, 18th July had been absolutely glorious. As the late afternoon shadows started to lengthen, I had decided to end a very happy day's photography with a couple of pictures taken from the grounds of Midford Castle where I always thought the scenic setting was one of the finest on the whole of the S & D. Two trains were due, 'W196', the 10.38 a.m. (SO) Manchester to Bournemouth, followed some twenty minutes later by '556', the 2.45 p.m. (SO) Bournemouth to Bristol.

Shortly after a quarter to five I saw in the distance the Midford Down Home signal come off, and a few minutes later a faint rumbling, and trembling of the ground warned me that 'W196' was about to appear from out of the cutting. To my pleasure, the train was hauled by two of the S & D's own 4Fs, Nos. 44559 and 44561, built for the line in 1922 by Armstrong Whitworth & Co. Note that in 1953, both engines still had their original Midland-type 'coal rail' tenders.

18th July, 1953

133. 'W196' was running a few minutes late and the 2.45 p.m. from Bournemouth must have been waiting at Midford Up Outer Home signal for the single line into Bath Junction, for no sooner had the two 4Fs and their train disappeared round the hillside in the distance, than the up train came into view. 2P No. 40563 and 4F No. 44422 were in charge of the express, and lit by the late afternoon sunshine, they made a lovely sight as they climbed up past the grounds of Midford Castle towards Combe Down Tunnel.

18th July, 1953

134.

2P No. 40696 and 'Battle of Britain' Pacific No. 34109 "Sir Trafford Leigh Mallory", both blowing off furiously, come charging up the bank from Midford station with the 8.05 a.m. (SO) Bournemouth to Sheffield. Judging by the speed at which they were travelling, both footplate crews obviously had the same intention—to spend as little time as possible in the notorious mile-long, Combe Down Tunnel!

25th July, 1953

135. 4F No. 44102 and 'Black Five' No. 44830 running south from Midford with the 7.43 a.m. (SO) Birmingham to Bournemouth.

25th July, 1953

THE 7Fs IN ACTION ON PASSENGER AND FREIGHT TRAINS

136. 2P No. 40697 and 7F No. 53802 swinging through the reverse curves towards Midford with a twelve-coach relief for Sheffield. (8.25 a.m. off Bournemouth.)

11th July, 1953

137. One week later, the same pair of engines, 2P No. 40697 and 7F No. 53802, head south from Midford with the 10.30 a.m. (SO) Liverpool to Bournemouth. In 1953 this train was scheduled to run for four Saturdays, starting on 18th July and ending on 8th August.

18th July, 1953

138. A 7F on her normal duties—No. 53805 draws near to Midford with an up goods. Note the tablet catcher arm extended to pick up at Midford the token for the single line section into Bath Junction.

6th June, 1953

139. On Saturday, 25th July, a relief for the North again left Bournemouth at 8.25 a.m. (see picture 136). This time the destination was Clitheroe, and with only ten on, large-boilered 7F No. 53807 had taken the train over the Mendips on her own. The 7F is seen here about to bring her train to a stand at Midford Up Outer Home signal, where she was booked to wait from 10.55 to 11.02 a.m. whilst a down relief ex-Walsall (due off Bath 10.43 a.m.) occupied the single line section between Bath Junction and Midford. In the event, 53807 was held for over ten minutes due to the late-running of the relief from Walsall.

25th July, 1953

140. On a fine afternoon in late spring, 2P No. 40563 and 'Black Five' No. 44826 climb up through the deep cutting towards Chilcompton Tunnel with the down "Pines". Driver Arthur Clist is in charge of 44826 which must have been steaming well to be blowing off after over three miles of continuous climbing on a ruling gradient of 1 in 50.

25th May, 1953

CHILCOMPTON TUNNEL

In the climb up the northern slopes of the Mendips, the S & D passed through Chilcompton Tunnel, which was 66 yards long, and lay just over one mile south of Midsomer Norton station. The approach to the tunnel was in a deep cutting through which the line climbed at 1 in 53, which had been the ruling gradient all the way up from Midsomer Norton.

141. Ivatt class 4MT 2-6-0 No. 43036 and 4F 0-6-0 No. 44096 dart out of the tunnel as they run swiftly downhill with the 2.45 p.m. (SO) Bournemouth to Bristol. (Disregard the reporting number 213. This referred to a down train which the 2-6-0 had helped (?) to take south in the morning.)

4th July, 1953

142. 2P No. 40634 and 'West Country' Pacific No. 34095 "Brentor" about to enter the tunnel with the 7.45 a.m. (SO) Bradford to Bournemouth.

4th July, 1953

143. 4F No. 44102 and 'Black Five' No. 44826 emerge from the southern end of Chilcompton Tunnel with the 9.40 a.m. (SO) Sheffield to Bournemouth.

1st August, 1953

144. 2P No. 40568 arrives with the 4.37 p.m. down stopping train from Bath.

2nd May, 1953

BINEGAR

The attractive, small station at Binegar was similar in design and layout to other stations built on the Bath extension of the Somerset and Dorset. Under Norman Down, station master at Binegar from 1944 until the closure of the S & D in 1966, Binegar station was always kept neat and tidy, and in 1953 it was awarded second prize in the competition for the 'Best Kept Station'. (In my opinion, only the profusion of flowers at the winning station, a little further up the line, robbed Binegar of first prize.)

145. Norman Down, station master at Binegar for 22 years from 1944 until the line's sad closure in 1966.

18th July, 1953

146. Engineers Special! A motorised P.W. trolley trundles through Binegar. The driver (in cap) is Dick Symes and his companion (wearing trilby) is lengthman Bill Prior. The third person on board was an 'unauthorised passenger' who had missed the up local train and was being given a lift—together with his two suitcases! The sort of kindly gesture which typified the S & D.

Note that although this was 1953—some 23 years since the S & D had been taken over by the L.M.S. and S.R., not to mention 5½ years after the railways of Britain had been nationalised—the trolley still bears the legend S & D J R !

18th July, 1953

147. A BULLEID PACIFIC IN DISGRACE!

On the morning of 1st August, when nearing Masbury Summit with a down train, Bulleid Pacific No. 34041 "Wilton" suddenly came to a grinding halt, her chain-driven valve gear in total disarray. The engine could be moved neither forwards nor backwards and was a complete failure. The Binegar station master, Norman Down, quickly assessed the situation, and used the pilot engine from a following express to draw "Wilton" and her train back down to Binegar where the Pacific was bundled into a siding and the pilot then worked "Wilton's" train forward. The whole movement was carried out smoothly and efficiently, but even so, by the time traffic was moving again, down trains were running over one hour late. The effect on up trains was equally disastrous, for the late-running of the down trains completely ruined the carefully worked out crossings with the up trains on the single line sections. —And all this on the busiest day of the year for the S & D!

During the morning, foreman fitter George Adams and a mate had come out from Bath shed to take down the Pacific's valve gear—or what was left of it! Then in the late afternoon, when the hectic flow of traffic over the S & D had at last started to die down, 'Black Five' No. 44839 arrived on the scene to tow the Pacific back to Bath shed. In this picture they are seen waiting for 'line clear', before crossing over onto the up road and setting off for Bath.

1st August, 1953

148.   Signalman L.G. Richards on duty in Binegar signal box, where everything was kept spotless and shining like a new pin.

2nd May, 1953

SHEPTON MALLET
The 7.43 a.m. (SO) Birmingham to Bournemouth

In 1953, as in previous years, the 7.43 a.m. (SO) Birmingham to Bournemouth (10.32 a.m. off Bath) had the distinction of being the only train over the Somerset and Dorset not booked to stop at Evercreech Junction. She had a five minute stop (11.19—11.24) at Shepton Mallet for water, and then ran non-stop to Wincanton, where there was a brief two minute call, before continuing on to Templecombe Upper.

On 18th July the train was taken over at Bath by large-boilered 7F No. 53807, and with a load of only eight coaches, she needed no assistance. However, coupled ahead of her (to save finding a separate light engine path) was 2P No. 40697 which was booked to run from Bath down to Evercreech Junction to assist the 11.12 a.m. (SO) Bournemouth to Derby.

The following three pictures show the sequence of events at Shepton Mallet.

149. After a swift descent from Masbury Summit, the train makes a careful approach to Shepton Mallet station for the 7F to stop beside the water column.

18th July, 1953

150. Whilst 53807 takes water, the 2P has uncoupled and drawn ahead prior to setting back into a siding off the down road.

18th July, 1953

151. With her tender replenished, 53807 sets off past 40697 for the run to Wincanton. Shortly afterwards, the 2P also departed south, running light engine down to Evercreech Junction.

18th July, 1953

152.

About one hour later, another large-boilered 7F rolled into Shepton Mallet station. This time it was No. 53806 in charge of the 10.35 a.m. (SO) Bournemouth to Manchester, and with twelve on, she had the assistance of 2P No. 40696. Incidentally, disregard the 2P's reporting number. '132' referred to a southbound train in the early hours of the morning–the 10.39 p.m. (Fridays only) Manchester to Bournemouth (4.10 a.m. off Bath)–which presumably 40696 had assisted. *18th July, 1953*

153. Because it has been reproduced before, many people will already know this picture, but it is of such a rare subject that I felt the year 1953 would not be complete without it. Two S & D 7F 2-8-0s on a passenger train was a very rare sight, but even more so when small- and large-boilered versions were together 'in a double-harness'. Unlike the only other time I ever saw this combination (pictures 114 and 115), this was a case of genuine double-heading. The train, seen here climbing towards Shepton Mallet, was the 10.05 a.m. (SO) Bournemouth to Cleethorpes, and with twelve on, small-boilered No. 53802 definitely needed the assistance of her younger sister, large-boilered No. 53808.

18th July, 1953

PRESTLEIGH

The climb up the southern slopes of the Mendips commenced immediately from the platform end at Evercreech Junction station. Apart from a very brief easing to 1 in 300 through Evercreech New station the gradient kept to an unbroken 1 in 50 for more than three miles as the line climbed up past Prestleigh and on towards Shepton Mallet.

154. Elderly 3F 0-6-0 No. 43204—originally S & D J R No. 65, built at Derby in 1896—and 2P No. 40700 pass underneath a farm bridge as they climb northwards from Prestleigh with an up stopping train.

1st August, 1953

155. 7F No. 53810—one of the 1925 series rebuilt with a small boiler—coming steadily up the long stretch of 1 in 50 past Prestleigh with a ten-coach relief from Bournemouth to the North.

1st August, 1953

The S & D 7Fs with ten on—two more coaches than either the Stanier 'Black Fives' or the Bulleid Pacifics were able to take over the Mendips on their own.

156. Large-boilered 7F No. 53806 coping manfully near Prestleigh with the 12.20 p.m. (SO) relief, Bournemouth to Walsall, made up of ten ex-L.N.E.R. coaches. This heavy stock, filled to capacity, must have been well over the maximum load of 310 tons laid down for an S&D 7F to take over Masbury Summit unassisted. I was so impressed with the way the engine was performing with this very heavy train, that I leapt into my car and dashed up to Masbury for a second shot of her nearing the summit. (See picture 120 in my book "The Somerset and Dorset—an English Cross-Country Railway.")

15th August, 1953

157. 7F No. 53810, with the 4.15 p.m. up stopping train from Templecombe, sets off from Evercreech Junction at 4.43 p.m. for the run up to Bath. Standing in the middle road, waiting for the platform to become free, is 3F No. 43218 with the stock for the 4.48 p.m. local from Evercreech Junction up the branch to Highbridge.

8th August, 1953

158. Three 2P 4-4-0s, Nos. 40697, 40634 and 40564, arrive, coupled together, from Templecombe to join the stud of pilot engines waiting to assist up expresses over the Mendips.

27th June, 1953

159.
However, as the middle road already contained four pilots, there wasn't room for all three new arrivals, so initially Nos. 40634 and 40697 had to be stabled in the station yard.

27th June, 1953

160. 2P No. 40563 and Bulleid Pacific No. 34042 "Dorchester", in charge of the 9.40 a.m. (SO) Sheffield to Bournemouth, drift cautiously round the very sharp curve by the North Box. On the right is one of the S & D backing signals. This was used during shunting operations to authorise a driver to draw back on the down main line, and then onto the branch, a freight train which had arrived from Bath.

8th August, 1953

161. Maximum effort! 4F No. 44422 climbs away from Evercreech Junction with an eight-coach relief from Bournemouth to Stoke—and no pilot! The eight coaches, filled to capacity, must have been over 20 tons above the 240 tons limit laid down for a 4F 0-6-0 to take over the Mendips, unassisted. But when the train ran in from Bournemouth, Evercreech Junction had no assisting engine available. The weather was fine, and 44422 in good shape, so, in typical S & D fashion, the crew said, "Right. We will go on our own." From the North Box one could see the line in the far distance, climbing up past Prestleigh. Not so many minutes later there was 44422, black smoke towering from her chimney, plodding steadily up the long stretch of 1 in 50 towards Shepton Mallet. Not only did 44422 and her gallant crew make it all right up to Masbury, but they were only a few minutes down on schedule as they breasted the summit. Happily 44422 is still 'alive', preserved by the North Staffordshire Railway Society.

8th August, 1953

162. Driver Charlie King poses with the four Johnson tanks which he had gone to so much trouble to position specially for me to be able to take this picture.

HIGHBRIDGE SHED
—on Sunday morning, 9th August, 1953

Whilst I was on holiday at Burnham-on-Sea in August, 1953, my friend driver Charlie King got permission for me to visit Highbridge shed on Sunday morning, 9th August. It was arranged that I would be shown round by Charlie, although he was not on duty that day. What I did *not* know was that Charlie King had sought, and been granted, permission by the shed foreman, to move any engine into a 'suitable photographic position' for me! No trains ran over the branch on a Sunday except for two milk workings in the afternoon, so when we arrived at the shed about 11 a.m., everything was peaceful and quiet. The only engine in steam was 3F No. 43218—old No. 73, built for the S & D J R in 1902 by Neilson, Reid & Co.—which was to work the afternoon milk. She stood beside the water tower: the Johnson tanks were all in 'unphotographable' positions. Charlie had brought with him a young friend, John Madeley, 'to assist in the manoeuvres'. "Right", said Charlie, climbing aboard the 3F, "Now where would you like the tanks placed?" For the next hour, Charlie King and John Madeley pushed and pulled Johnson tanks in all directions, eventually getting them set out in a 'fan' as seen in picture 162. For me, the whole morning was tremendous fun, and all the pictures on these two pages I owe to Charlie's great kindness. It was typical of him to have gone to so much trouble, not to mention hard work, on my behalf, for he was one of the most kind-hearted and friendly drivers on the S & D.

Charlie King died in July, 1979. His passing brought sadness not only to his fellow railwaymen, but also to many railway enthusiasts to whom he had always been such a very good friend.

163. Driver Charlie King and John Madeley.

164. —And the 3F 0-6-0 No. 43218 which Charlie used to haul the Johnson tanks into position for picture 162.

171. No. 73050, one of three brand new B.R. standard class 5 4-6-0s allocated to the Somerset and Dorset. The new engine is seen here on Bath shed shortly after her arrival from London where she had been taking part in the International Railway Congress Association Exhibition at Willesden before being delivered to Bath Motive Power Depot. No. 73050 had been given a special exhibition finish and was absolutely immaculate. Driver Arthur Clist and his fireman, proud of their new mount, are looking out happily from the cab.

19th June, 1954

BATH MOTIVE POWER DEPOT

172. S & D 7F 2-8-0 No. 53807, one of the 1925 series, standing beside Bath M.P.D.'s new brick-built coaling stage which had recently replaced an earlier coaling stage of wooden construction, built in 1884. No. 53807 had arrived back from Derby the previous month after an overhaul which included the replacement of her large boiler with one of the smaller G9AS type of 4 ft. 9$\frac{1}{8}$ in. diameter.

24th July, 1954

173.

Driver Donald Beale standing in front of S.R. Pacific No. 34043 "Combe Martin". With the arrival of the Standard class 5 4-6-0s, Bath's S.R. Pacifics were returned to the Southern Region, "Combe Martin" going to Bournemouth shed (71B).

19th June, 1954

174. One of the Somerset and Dorset's S.R. 'West Country' Pacifics, No. 34040 "Crewkerne", prepares to stop at Midsomer Norton with the 9.55 a.m. down semi-fast from Bath (9.05 a.m. ex-Bristol).

30th January, 1954

A WINTRY START TO THE YEAR

Quite heavy falls of snow covered Somerset in late January and early February.

175. The 12.35 p.m. down freight to Evercreech Junction coming up the bank out of Bath, hauled by S & D 7F No. 53803 and banked in the rear by a 4F 0-6-0.

3rd February, 1954

176. S & D 7F No. 53802, in charge of the 12.35 p.m. Bath—Evercreech Junction goods, running briskly downhill towards Midford.

27th January, 1954

177. On a beautiful but bitterly cold morning in late January, S & D 7F No. 53806—one of the large boilered 1925 series—climbs vigorously uphill towards Binegar with the 10.45 a.m. Midsomer Norton—Evercreech Junction coal train. Giving hearty assistance in the rear is 3F 0-6-0T No. 47557.

30th January, 1954

178. The Wednesday of the first week—U class No. 31621 drops down the bank into Bath with the 11.40 a.m. from Bournemouth, specially made up to eight coaches for the test.

3rd March, 1954

THE S.R. U AND U1 TRIALS

During the first fortnight in March, the Southern Region carried out a series of test runs over the Somerset and Dorset with U and U1 class 2-6-0s to assess their suitability for use over the line. The trains worked were the 11.40 a.m. up from Bournemouth and the 4.25 p.m. down from Bath. On the Mondays, Tuesdays and Wednesdays the load was eight coaches, and for the latter half of each week this was increased to twelve, with assistance being given between Bath and Evercreech Junction for the climb over the Mendips.

U class No. 31621 worked the test trains during the first week, followed by U1 class No. 31906 for the second week.

179. Driver Vic Williams and fireman Basil Foot who were in charge of the U between Templecombe and Bath.

6th March, 1954

180. The Thursday of the first week—the 11.40 a.m. from Bournemouth comes in over Bath Junction. With the load now made up to twelve coaches, U class No. 31621 had had the assistance of 2P No. 40634 from Evercreech Junction for the climb over the Mendips.

4th March, 1954

181. The Tuesday of the second week—U1 class No. 31906 appears through the gloom of a miserable day and rumbles over the river bridge with the 11.40 a.m. up from Bournemouth as she makes a cautious approach into Bath, Green Park, terminus.

9th March, 1954

182. The crew of the U1 between Templecombe and Bath—Driver Len Dutton and fireman John Wood.
13th March, 1954

183. The Thursday of the second week—2P No. 40563 and U1 No. 31906 emerge from Devonshire Tunnel into weak winter sunshine with the twelve-coach 11.40 a.m. from Bournemouth.
11th March, 1954

A SOUTHERN "SCHOOLS" CLASS ON THE SOMERSET AND DORSET

In late April the S & D had a most interesting visitor—one of the Southern's outstanding "Schools" class 4-4-0s. The engine was hauling an enthusiasts' excursion which ran from Waterloo to Bournemouth, then up the S & D to Bath, and finally from Bath down to Templecombe and back to London over the ex-L & S.W.R. West of England main line. Apart from the run from Bath down to Templecombe, the train was worked throughout by the "Schools", with a second engine giving assistance for the run over the S & D from Bournemouth up to Bath. The original intention was that the assisting engine should be an ex-L & S.W.R. T9 4-4-0. At the last moment however, trouble was experienced with the fitting of a mechanical tablet catcher to the T9 (which was to be the train engine) and a rather grubby ex-L.M.S. 2P had to be hastily substituted.

This is thought to have been only the third time a "Schools" ran over the Somerset and Dorset. The two previous occasions had apparently been with troop trains during the War.

184. "Schools" class No. 30932 "Blundells" and 2P No. 40601 coast in over the level crossing and past the tall South Box as they arrive at Evercreech Junction with the excursion.

25th April, 1954

185. The ex-S.R. and ex-L.M.S.R. 4-4-0s standing with their train in Evercreech Junction station.

25th April, 1954

186. The excursion passing over Masbury Summit. The two engines had made an excellent climb up the southern slopes of the Mendips, and breasted the summit in fine style.

25th April, 1954

187. Masbury Summit is left behind, and all is set for a swift descent down the 7½ miles to Radstock.

Note the 2nd class coach next to the engine. This was most unusual because in 1954, and for many years before, there had been only two classes of travel on British railways—'First' and 'Third'. However, 'Second' class was in general use in Europe, so for continental travellers 'Second' class coaches were included in the boat trains to and from Dover and Folkestone. This particular coach, S4432S, was one of a batch of 20 built to Maunsell's design in 1933. They were known as 'nondescript brakes' because they had slots for a sign that could be reversed, which said 'First' on one side, and 'Second' on the other, and could be altered according to demand for accommodation.

25th April, 1954

THE S & D's NEW CLASS 5s

In the late spring of 1954, three brand new B.R. Standard class 5 4-6-0s, Nos. 73050, 73051 and 73052, were allocated to Bath M.P.D. The engines were built at Derby, 73050 being completed in April, and 73051/2 in May. The first engines to be delivered to Bath M.P.D. were 73051/2 which arrived towards the end of May. 73050, although completed earlier than her two sisters, did not appear on the S & D scene until June. This was because she had been sent straight from Derby to London to take part in the International Railway Congress Exhibition at Willesden, before starting work on the S & D.

188. The crew of No. 73051, driver Arthur Turner (right) and fireman David Massey, stand in front of their new Standard class 5.
7th June, 1954

190. The first run over the S & D by one of the new class 5s was on 29th May when No. 73051 hauled the 3.35 p.m. from Bournemouth up to Bath. (The engine had worked light engine, from Derby down to Bournemouth via Brent, Willesden, Feltham and Basingstoke.) Driver Walt Jeans was in charge of 73051, and the train is seen here running in to Shepton Mallet.

29th May, 1954

189. The maker's plate of No. 7305

191. No. 73050 pilots No. 34042 "Dorchester"—one of the Southern Pacifics she had displaced from Bath M.P.D.—through the reverse curves towards Midford with the 2.45 p.m. (SO) Bournemouth to Bristol.

21st August, 1954

192. The third of Bath's new Standard class 5s, No. 73052, assisted by 4F No. 44422, climbs away southwards from Midford with the 7.43 a.m. (SO) Birmingham to Bournemouth. The down express, running some ten minutes late, had delayed the 6.50 a.m. up stopping train from Bournemouth which is seen standing at Midford's Up Outer Home signal, waiting for the single line into Bath Junction to become clear.

28th August, 1954

S & D 7F No. 53807

In June S & D 7F No. 53807 returned from a general overhaul at Derby which included the replacement of her large boiler with one of the smaller G9AS type of 4 ft. $9\frac{1}{8}$ in. diameter. During the reconditioning of the engine it was found that the smokebox saddle had deteriorated to the extent that the usual procedure of fitting a 'distance-piece' to accommodate the smaller diameter of the new boiler could not be followed. So 53807 was given a new one-piece smokebox saddle, and this made her unique and immediately recognisable from her ten sisters, for she was the only S & D 7F to have a small boiler, one-piece smokebox saddle, and the ejector gear on the left hand side of the smokebox. (Being a left-hand drive engine.)

193. A few days after her return from Derby, No. 53807 was put in charge of the 7.18 p.m. down goods from Bath to Templecombe upper yard. It was a glorious June evening, and I followed the train by car, taking many pictures of 53807 as she wended her way southwards. In this final picture, taken just before sunset, 53807 is bringing her train up the 1 in 50 towards Chilcompton—ably assisted by a 'Jinty' banking diligently in the rear.

22nd June, 1954

THE CENTENARY OF THE SOMERSET CENTRAL RAILWAY

The Somerset Central Railway was opened on 28th August, 1854 and to celebrate the centenary a special excursion train was run from Glastonbury to Burnham-on-Sea and back. The train of twelve coaches was hauled by 3F No. 43201 — built for the S & D J R at Derby in 1896 — and for the event she carried her original number, 64, and the letters S & D J R on her buffer beam and tender sides.

195. The centenary special arriving back at Glastonbury in the early evening. The crew for the return run was driver Bill Peck and fireman Maurice Cook.

28th August, 1954

196. No. 43201, bedecked in bunting, stands at the east end of Glastonbury station after the return run from Burnham-on-Sea. Glastonbury Tor may just be discerned on the distant hilltop.

28th August, 1954

194. (Left) The conditions when I took this photograph of No. 53807 nearing Masbury Summit, were in sharp contrast to the beautiful, still, June evening of the picture above, for it was early on a bitterly cold Sunday morning in mid February and a near gale force east wind was sweeping across the high Mendips. No. 53807 — then still with her large boiler — was taking part in some goods train test runs between Bath and Evercreech Junction and back. The S & D, normally closed between Bath and Evercreech Junction on Sundays, had been specially opened for the tests so as not to interfere with normal weekday traffic. Driver Bert Read was in charge of 53807, and also on the footplate was Inspector Jack Hookey, both of whom can be seen looking out of the cab as 53807 comes up to the 811 ft. summit with her test train of forty-two 13T. wagons of class 3 traffic.

14th February, 1954

197. Two freight locomotives, 3F No. 43441 and 7F No. 53807, come storming up the 1 in 50 bank out of Bath in fine style with the 9.18 a.m. (SO) Birmingham to Bournemouth (12.00 noon off Bath).

11th September, 1954

THE S & D 7F 2-8-0s ON PASSENGER TRAINS

Once again, as in the previous four years, intense traffic on Saturdays at the height of the summer service left no alternative but for the 7Fs to be used on passenger trains.

198. 7F No. 53801 sets off from Cole with the 4.15 p.m. up stopping train from Templecombe.

14th August, 1954

199. A passenger train double-headed by two S & D 7F 2-8-0s was a very rare sight—but this train, seen approaching Evercreech Junction in the early evening, is not quite what it appears to be! In this instance the train hauled by 7Fs Nos. 53807 and 53805 is an up empty stock working which had left Bournemouth West at 4.10 p.m.

11th September, 1954

200. After 7F No. 53807's return from Derby in June, fitted with a small boiler, only one S & D 7F, No. 53806, still retained a large boiler. She is seen here, piloted by 2P No. 40698, swinging through the reverse curves towards Midford with the 10.35 a.m. (SO) Bournemouth to Manchester.

28th August, 1954

201. BOURNEMOUTH WEST. One of the S & D's new B.R. class 5s, No. 73052—only just over three months old—sets off from Bournemouth West in the early evening with the 6.40 p.m. for Bath.

7th August, 1954

202. BROADSTONE BANK. The S & D's last big-boilered 7F 2-8-0, No. 53806, climbing in very determined style up the two miles of 1 in 75 towards Broadstone with the 12.25 p.m. (SO) Bournemouth to Birmingham.

7th August, 1954

203. BROADSTONE. The 10.05 a.m. (SO) Bournemouth to Cleethorpes, hauled by S & D 7F No. 53807, leaves the Southern line at Broadstone and turns north on to the Somerset and Dorset single line to Corfe Mullen.

7th August, 1954

204. For the first eight miles of their journey from Bournemouth to Bath, S & D trains ran over Southern lines. The Somerset and Dorset's own track commenced at Broadstone, starting with a 3-mile single line section as far as Corfe Mullen. 4F No. 44561 has just swung north at Broadstone on to the S & D with the 3.35 p.m. from Bournemouth—the 'Up Mail'—and is climbing the 1 in 97 bank past Broadstone golf course on her way towards Corfe Mullen.

7th August, 1954

TEMPLECOMBE

205. B.R. class 5 No. 73050, with the road clear for her to run up the spur to Templecombe Upper Station approaches Templecombe Junction with the 7.43 a.m. (SO) Birmingham to Bournemouth. Note the unusual design of Whitaker tablet catching apparatus set between the up and down roads. This type of apparatus was used wherever there was limited clearance, the pick-up arm being designed to fall down out of the way as soon as it had received the tablet.

31st July, 1954

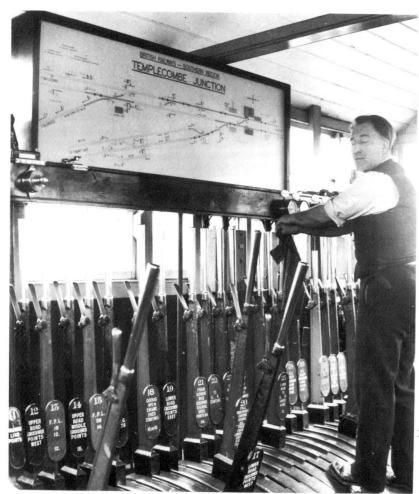

206. Signalman Vivian on duty in Templecombe Junction Box.

31st July, 1954

207. 7F No. 53804, in charge of the 10.05 a.m. (SO) Bournemouth to Cleethorpes, sweeps up the sharp rise to Templecombe No. 2 Junction.

31st July, 1954

208. Ivatt 2-6-2T No. 41249 comes past Templecombe shed, rebuilt in 1950, with the 4.45 p.m. Bailey Gate– Templecombe milk train.

31st July, 1954

209. 3F 0-6-0 No. 43201 and 1P 0-4-4T No. 58073 shunting stock in the Lower Yard, to form a local train for Highbridge.

31st July, 1954

COLE

210. 3F 0-6-0 No. 43436 passes over the ex-Great Western West of England main line, as she draws near to Cole with the afternoon Bason Bridge—Templecombe milk train.

14th August, 1954

211. 2P No. 40634 and S.R. Pacific No. 34040 "Crewkerne", running fast towards Cole, sweep round the curve over Cole viaduct with the 7.50 a.m. (SO) Bradford to Bournemouth.

14th August, 1954

WINSOR HILL

As the Somerset and Dorset approached Winsor Hill, the up and down lines diverged to pass through separate tunnels some distance apart from each other. This unusual feature came about when the original single line was doubled in 1892. By deviating a short distance to the west, it was found possible to make the tunnel for the new (up) line 110 yards shorter than the original tunnel of 242 yards used by the down line. Situated between the up and down lines just north of the twin tunnels was Winsor Hill signal box—the only box on the S & D built entirely of stone—which controlled the entrances to sidings serving quarries situated on either side of the line. Both quarries ceased working soon after the end of the Second World War, and Winsor Hill Box was closed in 1948.

212. The up "Pines Express", hauled by 2P No. 40697 and S.R. Pacific No. 34042 "Dorchester", emerges from the north end of the tunnel and passes by the closed and derelict Winsor Hill signal box.

18th September, 1954

213. S & D 7F No. 53805 drifts downhill out of Winsor Hill Tunnel with the 10.45 a.m. down coal train from Midsomer Norton.

27th March, 1954

CHILCOMPTON TUNNEL

214. (Above) S & D 7F No. 53810, working extremely hard, bursts out of Chilcompton Tunnel as she labours uphill at the head of the heavy 10.45 a.m. down coal train from Midsomer Norton.

10th April, 1954

215. To be followed by 'Jinty' 3F tank No. 47496 working equally hard at the rear of the train.

10th April, 1954

216. 2P 4-4-0 No. 40696, in charge of an up local, sweeps out of the
northern end of the tunnel and down the steep bank towards
Midsomer Norton.

27th March, 1954

217. On a hot afternoon in June, two ex-S & D J R 4F 0-6-0s Nos.
44559 and 44560, come plodding uphill towards Chilcompton
Tunnel with the 10.38 a.m. (SO) Manchester to Bournemouth.

19th June, 1954

WELLOW

218. The 6.05 p.m. (SX) Bath–Binegar local, hauled by 'Jinty' 3F tank No. 47465, pauses briefly at Wellow. Normally this train was worked by an Ivatt 2-6-2T, but on this particular evening, no 2-6-2T was available, so the 'Jinty' was pressed into service.

12th April, 1954

219. 4F No. 44417 runs in with the 3.15 p.m. down stopping train from Bath.
20th March, 1954

SOUTH OF MIDFORD

220. With regulators closed, ex-M.R. 2P No. 40527, driven by Bill Gunning, and S.R. Pacific No. 34043 "Combe Martin", come drifting round the curve towards Midford with the 10.05 a.m. (SO) Bournemouth to Cleethorpes. The Up Distant signal had been 'on', and they were preparing to find the Midford Up Outer Home signal against them. (Which it was!) The ex-Midland 2P had been transferred to the S & D as a replacement for sister engine No. 40505 which had been withdrawn from service the previous winter.

28th August, 1954

221. The 10.38 a.m. (SO) Manchester to Bournemouth, hauled by two 4F 0-6-0s, Nos. 44559 and 44560—both built for the S & D.J.R. in 1922—sweeps southwards off Midford viaduct and onto double track which would last for the next 32 miles as far as Templecombe.

21st August, 1954

222.　The down "Pines Express", hauled by 2P No. 40634 and S.R. Pacific No. 34042 "Dorchester", leaves Combe Down Tunnel and drifts downhill over Tucking Mill viaduct towards Midford.

10th April, 1954

HORSECOMBE VALE

223.　4F No. 44096 and 2P No. 40697 climbing towards Combe Down Tunnel with the 12.55 p.m. up stopping train from Bournemouth.

21st August, 1954

COMBE DOWN TUNNEL

224. The up "Pines Express", hauled by 2P No. 40563 and S.R. Pacific No. 34042 "Dorchester", leaves Combe Down Tunnel and starts the steep descent into Bath.

1st May, 1954

225.

S.R. Pacific No. 34041 "Wilton" emerges from the tunnel into Lyncombe Vale with the up "Pines" Relief.

1st May, 1954

BATH JUNCTION

226. Ex-M.R. 2P No. 40527 and S.R. Pacific No. 34042 "Dorchester", in charge of the 9.25 a.m. (SO) Bournemouth to Manchester and Liverpool, drift down off the Somerset and Dorset single line from Midford to join the Midland line at Bath Junction for the final half-mile into Bath, Green Park, station.

19th June, 1954

227. After a careful approach to the Junction, S & D 7F No. 53805 runs in on the goods loop with the 6.05 a.m. up freight from Templecombe. When 53805 had brought her train to a stand, the 'Jinty' on the left, No. 47465, drew forward and coupled on to the rear. Then as soon as the 7F had uncoupled and drawn forward out of the way, the 'Jinty' began shunting the wagons into the goods yard. Driver Charlie Brown is on 47465, with driver Ted Smith on 53805.

27th February, 1954

228. (Above) On setting off from Bath station, S & D trains had a half-mile run on the level over the Midland line before swinging south at Bath Junction on to the Somerset and Dorset and the start of the climb out of Bath. As 2P No. 40697 and B.R. class 5 No. 73051 approached the Junction with the 9.18 a.m. (SO) Birmingham to Bournemouth, both engines were being driven very hard so as to get up as much speed as possible for the coming attack on the 1 in 50 bank out of Bath.

19th June, 1954

229. The 7.35 a.m. (SO) Nottingham to Bournemouth, hauled by a 2P and S.R. Pacific No. 34040 "Crewkerne", about to turn south at Bath Junction on to the Somerset and Dorset single line to Midford.

19th June, 1954

230. Activity at Bath, Green Park, on a bright winter's afternoon. S.R. Pacific No. 34043 "Combe Martin" is just getting under way with the 4.26 p.m. down semi-fast for Bournemouth, whilst in the middle road, 2P No. 40698 prepares to draw out the stock to form the 4.37 p.m. down stopping train to Templecombe. Green Park station was a 'mecca' for railway enthusiasts of all ages—the S & D always had so much to offer. I wonder if the two schoolboys on the right will see this picture and recognise themselves—they must now be nearing their 'forties!

13th February, 1954

BATH, GREEN PARK, STATION

231. Dave Hadfield, the driver of 2P No. 40563, prepares to bring the up "Pines Express" gently to a stand just short of the buffers in Bath, Green Park, station. The train engine is B.R. class 5 No. 73050, driven by Bert Brewer.

3rd July, 1954

The Somerset and Dorset in the 'Fifties

PART 2
1955~1959

MAXIMUM EFFORT. The 8.55 a.m. down goods has just emerged from Devonshire Tunnel, Bath, and is climbing up the 1 in 50 through Lyncombe Vale, hauled by S & D 7F 2-8-0 No. 53805 and banked in the rear by a 4F 0-6-0.

7th May, 1955

THE SPIRIT OF THE SOMERSET AND DORSET

It was a tradition with S & D enginemen that a late arrival at Bath of the down "Pines Express" was accepted as a challenge; if it was humanly possible, the endeavour would always be 'Right time Bournemouth'.

On 16th April 1955, waiting to take over the down "Pines Express" at Bath, were driver Donald Beale and fireman Frank Stickley with B.R. class 5 No. 73050. Coupled ahead of them to give assistance over the Mendips down to Evercreech Junction, was 2P No. 40564. Word had come through that the train was running behind time, and this was confirmed when the Station Box signalman slid back his window and called out to Donald "Twenty-five late Gloucester".

The eventual departure from Bath was 31 minutes behind schedule. Prior to setting off, Donald Beale had had a word with the crew of the 2P who assured him of their whole hearted co-operation. The run that followed was quite magnificent — all 31 minutes were regained, and only the frustration of a final signal check at Branksome cheated the crew of an arrival at Bournemouth West, 'Right time'.

I took this picture of the train nearing Binegar. Long before they appeared in sight, I had heard them coming! With exhausts rising nearly vertically, both engines were being worked close to all-out — and the sight and sound of "The Pines Express" as it tore past me were thrilling in the extreme. Their climb of the Mendips from Radstock up to Masbury Summit, 811 feet above sea level, must have been one of the fastest ever made.

16th April, 1955

The
Somerset and Dorset
in the 'Fifties

PART 2
1955~1959

by
Ivo Peters B.E.M.

Johnson 0-4-4T. No. 58072 enjoys a quiet boiler washout in the old Midland shed during her first weekend at Bath whilst on temporary loan from Highbridge M.P.D. Her companion on the left is 2P 4-4-0 No. 40696, built at Crewe in 1932.

30th April, 1955

INTRODUCTION

Part one of "The Somerset and Dorset in the 'Fifties" covered the period from 1950 to 1954. Part two now takes us from 1955 to 1959. During these five years, traffic over the Somerset and Dorset, both passenger and freight, kept up well, and to the railway enthusiast's delight, the constantly changing variety in motive power continued unabated. In fact by the end of the 'fifties, the only member of the pre-nationalisation 'Big Four' railway companies not represented on the S & D was the L.N.E.R.

But in 1958 an event occurred which was to have fatal consequences for the Somerset and Dorset – in a re-shuffle of regional boundaries the Western Region gained a dominating control over the line. Initially there was little to show for the change, and no hint given of the fate that was to befall this enchanting line. 1959 dawned with the S & D still an important and busy line, but as the year drew to a close, how many would have believed that the Somerset and Dorset had less than seven more years to live?

IVO PETERS
1981

The train times quoted throughout this book are from the Working Time Table. (SO) after a train time indicates that the train ran only on Saturdays during the summer service.

BRITISH RAILWAYS
SOMERSET & DORSET SECTION
NUMBERS AND CLASSES OF ENGINES 1ST. JANY. 1956.

POWER CLASS	MAKERS	TYPE AND WHEELS	SIZE OF CYLINDERS	WHEEL DIAMETERS CARRYING	WHEEL DIAMETERS COUPLED	BOILER PRESS	BRAKE	TANK CAP GALLONS	ENGINE NUMBERS			NO. OF ENGS.
2	SHARP STEWART AND CO.	PASSENGER TENDER 4-4-0	20½" x 26"	3'-6½"	7'-0½"	160	S.E.	3250	40509			1
2	M.R. CO. DERBY.	-DO-	-DO-	3'-6½"	7'-0½"	160	S.E.	3500	40527			1
2	L.M.S. DERBY.	-DO-	19" x 26"	3'-6½"	6'-9"	180	S.E.	3500	40563 40564 40568 / 40569 40601 40634			6
2	L.M.S. CREWE.	-DO-	19" x 26"	3'-6½"	6'-9"	180	S.E.	3500	40696 40697 40698 / 40700			4
2	L.M.R. CREWE.	MIXED TRAFF. TANK 2-6-2	16" x 24"	3'-0"	5'-0"	200	S.E.	1350	41241 41242 41243 / 41248 41249			5
3	M.R. CO. DERBY.	FREIGHT TDR. 0-6-0	18" x 26"	—	5'-3"	175	S.E.	2950 / 3250	43194 43201 / 43204			3
3	NEILSON REID AND CO.	" 0-6-0	18" x 26"	—	5'-3"	175	S.E.	2950 / 3250	43216 43248 / 43218			3
3	DUBS AND COMPANY.	" 0-6-0	18" x 26"	—	5'-3"	175	S.E.	3250	43356 43419 43436			3
4	KERR STUART AND CO.	" 0-6-0	20" x 26"	—	5'-3"	175	S.E.	3500	44096 44102			2
4	L.M.S. CREWE.	" 0-6-0	20" x 26"	—	5'-3"	175	S.E.	3500	44146 44523			2
4	L.M.S. DERBY.	" 0-6-0	20" x 26"	—	5'-3"	175	S.E.	3500	44417 44422			2
4	ARMSTRONG WHITWORTH AND CO.	" 0-6-0	20" x 26"	—	5'-3"	175	S.E.	3500	44557 44558 44559 / 44560 44561			5
5	L.M.S. CREWE.	MIXED TRAFF. TEND. 4-6-0	18½" x 28"	3'-3½"	6'-0"	225	S.E.	4000	44826 44830 44839 / 44917			4
5	ARMSTRONG WHITWORTH.	" " " 4-6-0	18½" x 28"	3'-3½"	6'-0"	225	S.E.	4000	45440			1
N.C	SENTINEL WAGON WORKS LIMITED.	SHUNTING TANK 0-4-0	6¾" x 9" (4)	—	3'-2"	275	S.	600	47190 47191			2
3	VULCAN FOUNDRY CO.	FREIGHT TANK 0-6-0	18" x 26"	—	4'-7"	160	S.E.	1200	47275 47496			2
3	W.G. BAGNELL LTD.	" 0-6-0	18" x 26"	—	4'-7"	160	S.E.	1200	47316 47465			2
3	HUNSLET ENGINE CO.	" 0-6-0	18" x 26"	—	4'-7"	160	S.E.	1200	47542 47557			2
7	M.R. CO. DERBY.	FREIGHT TDR. 2-8-0	21" x 28"	3'-3½"	4'-8½"	190	S.E.	3500	53800 53801 53802 / 53803 53804 53805			6
7	STEPHENSON AND CO.	" " 2-8-0	21" x 28"	3'-3½"	4'-8½"	190	S.E.	3500	53806 53807 53808 / 53809 53810			5
1	M.R. CO. DERBY.	PASSENGER TANK 0-4-4	18" x 24"	3'-1"	5'-4"	150	S.E.	1150	58051			1
1	NEILSON AND CO.	" " 0-4-4	18" x 24"	3'-1"	5'-4"	150	S.E.	1150	58072			1
1	DUBS AND CO.	" " 0-4-4	18" x 24"	3'-1"	5'-4"	150	S.E.	1150	58073			1
1	DUBS AND CO.	" " 0-4-4	18" x 24"	3'-1"	5'-4"	150	S.E.	1270	58086			1
											TOTAL	65

S.   STEAM BRAKE.

E.   VACUUM EJECTOR.

THE INFORMATION CONCERNING CLASS 5 4-6-0s
IS INCORRECT.
B.R. STANDARD CLASS 5s Nos. 73050, 73051 AND
73052 HAVE BEEN OMITTED.
STANIER 'BLACK FIVES' Nos. 44826, 44830
AND 44839 HAVE BEEN INCLUDED, BUT
WERE NO LONGER ALLOCATED TO THE S&D
ON 1ST JANUARY 1956.

BRITISH RAILWAYS
SOUTHERN REGION
M & E.E. DEPT.
LOCO DRAWING OFFICE
EASTLEIGH.

H.H. SWIFT.

E.49521.

1. A cold start to the year. S & D 4F 0-6-0 No. 44557 sets off from Binegar with the 3.15 p.m. down local from Bath to Templecombe.

26th February, 1955

1955

Early in the year a class of locomotive which had not previously run over the line, appeared on the S & D scene for the first time – the B.R. standard class 4 2-6-0. After the initial trial run up from Bournemouth on 5th March, engines of this class begun running regularly over the line. No B.R. standard class 4 2-6-0s were actually allocated to Bath M.P.D. – the engines working over the S & D came from Eastleigh shed (71A) which provided the motive power for the 12.55 p.m. up from Bournemouth (7.05 p.m. return from Bath).

In April Bath M.P.D. experienced a sudden but temporary shortage of tank engines, and this led to one of the elderly Johnson 0-4-4 tanks being hastily borrowed from Highbridge shed in order to work the 6.05 p.m. Bath – Binegar local (7.10 p.m. Binegar – Bath return) – the first time for many years that one of these attractive small tank engines had been used on the main line north of Evercreech Junction.

1955 was to see the end of the large-boilered variety of S & D 7F 2-8-0. At the start of the year only one of the 1925 series, No. 53806, still retained a large diameter boiler, but in late autumn she went to Derby for a general overhaul which included the replacement of her large boiler by one of the smaller G9AS type of 4′ 9$^{1}/_{8}$″ diameter. So from then on, all eleven engines of the class had small boilers – and sadly the sight of one of the handsome S & D large-boilered 2-8-0s had vanished for ever from the Somerset and Dorset scene.

2. 7F No. 53806, the last of the S & D 2-8-0s to retain a large boiler, coasting downhill towards Moorewood with the 4.45 p.m. up goods from Evercreech Junction.
16th April, 1955

NEWCOMERS
ON BATH SHED

3. For the duration of the summer service, Bath had the benefit of two additional B.R. class 5s, Nos. 73073 and 73074, on loan from Patricroft. These engines differed from the S & D's own B.R. class 5s in having the larger type of BRIC tender. 73074 is seen here on Bath shed shortly after her arrival on the S & D.

7th May, 1955

4. B.R. standard class 4 2-6-0 No. 76012 standing outside the S & D shed at Bath after her first trial run up from Bournemouth.

5th March, 1955

5. Johnson 1P 0-4-4T. No. 58072, borrowed for a brief period from Highbridge to help out during a temporary shortage of tank engines at Bath, basks in the sunshine outside the old Midland shed.

7th May, 1955

6.
The initial trial run over the S & D by a B.R. standard class 4 2-6-0. No. 76012, piloted by 2P 4-4-0 No. 40568, climbs through Horsecombe Vale towards Combe Down Tunnel with the 11.40 a.m. up semi-fast from Bournemouth.
5th March, 1955

THE B.R. STANDARD CLASS 4 2-6-0s MAKE THEIR FIRST APPEARANCE ON THE SOMERSET AND DORSET

7. 76012's trial run over the S & D having gone off smoothly, Eastleigh commenced using this type for the 12.55 p.m. up from Bournemouth (7.05 p.m. return from Bath) — Eastleigh shed (71A) being responsible for providing the motive power for these workings. On a bright Saturday afternoon in early March, No. 76027 — not yet fitted with a tablet catcher — sets off from Evercreech Junction with the 12.55 p.m. up from Bournemouth.
12th March, 1955

8. Although directly descended from the ex-L.M.S. Ivatt class 4MT 2-6-0s — which, as originally designed with a double blastpipe and chimney, had performed so abysmally over the S & D — the B.R. standard class 4 2-6-0s were quickly accepted by S & D enginemen as good, reliable locomotives. Their use soon spread beyond the working of the 12.55 p.m. from Bournemouth; on a busy Saturday in late June No. 76025, piloted by 2P No. 40696, sweeps down-hill out of Chilcompton Tunnel with a summer Saturday relief from Bournemouth to the North.

25th June, 1955

9. — And the supreme accolade! No. 76012, with assistance from 2P No. 40569, is entrusted with "The Pines Express". Judging by the sound and fierceness of their exhausts, both engines — and their firemen! — were having to work very hard as they climbed up towards Chilcompton Tunnel with the Down "Pines Express". Without belittling the ability of these engines, the use of a standard class 4 2-6-0 on "The Pines Express" can only have indicated how extremely tight the locomotive situation must have been on the S & D on the first Saturday in August!

6th August, 1955

FOR THE FIRST TIME FOR MANY YEARS A JOHNSON 1P 0-4-4T. WORKS OVER THE MAIN LINE NORTH OF EVERCREECH JUNCTION

Towards the end of April, Bath M.P.D. found themselves suddenly short of tank engines, and arrangements were made to borrow for a short while, one of Highbridge shed's Johnson tanks. The visitor to Bath was No. 58072, built for the Midland Railway by Neilson & Co. towards the end of the last century. Note that she still retained the horizontal pipes running back from her smokebox, from the days when she was fitted with condensing apparatus for working through the Metropolitan tunnels in the London area — a far cry from her journeys through the tranquil Somerset countryside in 1955!

10.   One of the main duties for 58072 was to work the 6.05 p.m. (SX) Bath – Binegar local and the 7.10 p.m. Binegar – Bath return. With driver Vic Hunt in charge, 58072 is seen here after her arrival at Binegar, running round her train in preparation for the return run to Bath.

25th April, 1955

11.   On a beautiful evening in early May, 58072 pulls away from Midford for the continuation of her run out to Binegar with the 6.05 p.m. local from Bath.
2nd May, 1955

The 6.05 p.m. Bath – Binegar local did not run on Saturdays, so on her last Saturday at Bath – "For a bit of fun", as the shed foreman put it to me – 58072 was rostered to work the 12.20 p.m. local over to Bristol, Temple Meads, – a duty normally performed by an Ivatt 2-6-2T. 58072 had been specially 'spruced up' for the occasion, and her arrival at Temple Meads, where she became the cynosure of all eyes, caused quite a sensation. As the crew beamed happily out of their cab, the driver of a Great Western "Castle" standing on an adjacent road, called out "Where did you get her from, mate – out of the Ark?"

12. 58072 collects her three coaches from the middle road to form the 12.20 p.m. local over to Bristol, Temple Meads.

14th May, 1955

13. – and sets off from Bath, past S & D 7F 2-8-0 No. 53804.

14th May, 1955

THE EVENING LOCAL
FROM BATH TO BINEGAR

Every evening, except for Saturdays and Sundays, a local set off from Bath at 6.05 p.m. and ran down the line as far as Binegar, calling at all stations on the way. After arriving at Binegar at 6.57 p.m., the engine ran round her train and then departed at 7.10 p.m. on the return run to Bath.

14. Johnson 0-4-4T. No. 58072, manned by driver Vic Hunt and fireman Len Russell, about to set off from Bath with the 6.05 p.m. (SX) local to Binegar. This was the Johnson tank's first evening on this duty since her arrival at Bath on loan from Highbridge. (See previous page). The ex-Great Western diesel railcar standing in the platform behind the 6.05 p.m. Binegar, was to form the 6.18 p.m. local to Bristol.

25th April, 1955

15. The normal power for the 6.05 p.m. Bath — Binegar local was an Ivatt 2-6-2 tank. No. 41243, seen here in charge of the train, is pulling away from Midford station and onto the viaduct.

21st June, 1955

16. Just occasionally, a 'Jinty' 0-6-0 tank was used instead of an Ivatt 2-6-2T. In this picture, 'Jinty' No. 47275 has just left Midford and is climbing smartly up the 1 in 60 leading south from the viaduct.

9th May, 1955

17. Binegar Station. Johnson 0-4-4T. No. 58072, having run round her train, is ready to depart at 7.10 p.m. on the return run to Bath. Officially the train should have been positioned in the up platform, but in practice it usually set off from the down platform, crossing over immediately onto the up line via the trailing cross-over seen in picture 10. (With the Down Starter 'off', the signalman anticipated that driver Hunt was going to propel back, and then draw forward into the up platform. He didn't!)

25th April, 1955

18. No. 44422, one of the ex-L.M.S. engines built at Derby in 1927, drops down past Midford goods yard with the 12.35 p.m. freight from Bath to Evercreech Junction. Happily 44422 has been preserved and is being painstakingly restored by the North Staffordshire Railway Society. On the right is my faithful old Bentley which knew the S & D so well, I am sure she could have found her own way from Bath to Masbury Summit!

4th March, 1955

THE 4F 0-6-0s, THE 'MAIDS OF ALL WORK'

In 1955 the Somerset and Dorset had eleven 4F 0-6-0s, five built specially for the S & D.J.R in 1922, and six ex-L.M.S. engines. Although the class had certain drawbacks, they were useful general-purpose engines, and gave yeoman service to the Somerset and Dorset over many years.

19. Another of the Derby-built ex-L.M.S. 4Fs, No. 44417, assists Stanier 'Black Five' No. 45440 in the climb over the Mendips with the 10.30 a.m. (SO) Liverpool to Bournemouth. The pair are seen here about to enter Chilcompton Tunnel.

25th June, 1955

20. 4Fs in double-harness. Nos. 44557 and 44559, two of the 4Fs built for the S & D in 1922 by Armstrong Whitworth & Co., struggle up through Midsomer Norton station with the heavy 12-coach 10.38 a.m. (SO) Manchester to Bournemouth on an overcast Saturday in early August.

6th August, 1955

21.

"Don't look now, but I think my back tender wheels are off!" A visiting ex-Midland Railway 4F, No. 43853, which had brought in a train from the North, finds herself in an embarrassing position at the entrance to Bath S & D shed. Her tender wheels having become derailed on the only line leading out of the depot, she had effectively 'put the cork in the bottle' and prevented any movement either on or off shed for over half an hour!

14th May, 1955

THE 2P 4-4-0s

The S & D's allocation of 2P 4-4-0s in 1955 totalled 12 engines. Ten of these were the ex-L.M.S. standard type with 6 ft. 9 in. coupled wheels, one of which, No. 40634, had been built for the Somerset and Dorset in 1928, her S & D.J.R. number being 45. The remaining two engines were the more elderly ex-Midland Railway type with 7 ft. 0½ in. coupled wheels. In 1955 all twelve engines were continuing to give good, reliable service.

22. The up "Pines Express" comes swinging through the reverse curves towards Midford, hauled by one of the ex-L.M.S., Derby-built 2Ps, No. 40563, and S.R. "West Country" Pacific No. 34043 "Combe Martin".
13th August, 1955

23. With rain pouring down from a leaden sky, ex-M.R. 2P No. 40527 tops Masbury Summit at a rapid rate of knots with the 4.15 p.m. up stopping train from Templecombe. The crew were driver Bill Gunning and passed fireman Arthur Turner. I had been on Shepton Mallet platform as they ran in, and when they got the 'Right away', Arthur Turner called out, "Race you to Masbury Summit!" – and off they went, like a shot out of a gun! The very wet conditions prevented any high-speed motoring, and we virtually 'dead-heated' at the summit, but I just had time to leap out of my car and 'press the button' for this picture of them. Arthur told me later that they had been on full regulator and 45% cut-off – which is borne out by the near-vertical rise of the old girl's exhaust as she stormed over the summit!
2nd April, 1955

— AND MODERN 'SUPER POWER'

24. Four Southern Light Pacifics had been transferred to Bath M.P.D. in 1951, but these were returned to Eastleigh depot in 1954 when the S & D received three brand-new B.R. class 5s. During the Summer Service Bournemouth M.P.D. continued to provide Pacifics on Saturdays to help with the heavy flow of traffic over the S & D, but it was rare to see one of these engines on the line during the winter months. So it took me by surprise when, on the first Saturday in January, the down "Pines Express" was hauled, not by one, but by two Southern Pacifics! On a cold and gloomy winter's afternoon Nos. 34043 "Combe Martin" and 34107 "Blandford Forum" are seen with the down "Pines" just south of Radstock at the start of the 7½-mile climb up to Masbury Summit.

1st January, 1955

25. In contrast to the dreary winter's scene above, this picture was taken on a glorious, warm Saturday afternoon in high summer. B.R. class 5 No. 73052 and Stanier 'Black Five' No. 45440, in charge of the 2.45 p.m. (SO) Bournemouth to Bristol, are romping up the 1 in 55 through Horsecombe Vale towards Combe Down Tunnel. With only 8 on, 45440 could have handled the train comfortably on her own. 73052 was not there to assist, but had been coupled ahead of 45440 to work back to Bath and so save having to find a separate light engine path for her.

2nd July, 1955

"WEST-COUNTRY" PACIFICS FROM BOURNEMOUTH CENTRAL M.P.D. WORKING OVER THE S & D

The number of trains running over the Somerset and Dorset on Saturdays during the Summer Service was greater than could be handled by the S & D's own motive power. So Bournemouth Central M.P.D. came to the rescue and provided several of their Light Pacifics for working over the S & D up to Bath and back.

26. No. 34095 "Brentor", piloted by 2P No. 40700, climbs the 1 in 50 bank out of Bath with the 9.15 a.m. (SO) Birmingham to Bournemouth.
23rd July, 1955

27.
The 9.15 a.m. (SO) Birmingham to Bournemouth again, this time hauled by 2P No. 40696 and No. 34093 "Saunton", heading south from Midford on an overcast Saturday in August. Standing on the up road, waiting for the single line section into Bath Junction to become clear, are 2P No. 40564 and 'Black Five' No. 44821 with the 10.05 a.m. (SO) Bournemouth to Cleethorpes.
13th August, 1955

28. S & D 4F No. 44559 and No. 34044 "Woolacombe" climbing uphill at 1 in 50 south of Chilcompton with the 7.35 a.m. (SO) Nottingham to Bournemouth.

30th July, 1955

29. On a very hot Saturday afternoon in late July, 2P No. 40563 and No. 34043 "Combe Martin", in charge of the 7.50 a.m. (SO) Bradford to Bournemouth, toil up the long stretch of 1 in 53 towards Chilcompton Tunnel.

23rd July, 1955

THE SOMERSET AND DORSET 7F 2-8-0s

In 1955 all eleven engines of this class were in fine form and giving excellent service. By the start of the year all the 1925 series, with the exception of 53806, had been reboilered with the smaller diameter G9AS boiler.

30. On a sunny evening in early May, an up goods hauled by No. 53810 emerges from Combe Down Tunnel into the beautiful, wooded surroundings of Lyncombe Vale.

9th May, 1955

31. (Below) No. 53801, in charge of the 12.35 p.m. down goods, draws near to Combe Down Tunnel and the end of the climb out of Bath. The summit came just a few yards before the northern entrance to the tunnel.

3rd March, 1955

32. MORNING. The fireman places the single-line tablet in the exchange apparatus ready to be given up at Midford, as 53809 leaves Combe Down Tunnel and starts to drop down through Horsecombe Vale with the 8.55 a.m. Bath — Evercreech Junction goods.

19th March, 1955

**A BUSY DAY
FOR No. 53809**

33. AFTERNOON. 53809, on her second journey of the day down to Evercreech Junction, climbs southwards from Binegar towards Masbury Summit with the 4.05 p.m. down coal train from Midsomer Norton.

19th March, 1955

Happily this S & D 7F is still alive today. Saved from the scrapyard by Mr. Frank Beaumont, she has been meticulously restored to running order by a small, dedicated group of enthusiasts and is now kept, in immaculate condition, at the Midland Railway Trust at Butterley, near Derby.

34. No. 53807, one of the reboilered 1925 series, taking water at Shepton Mallet whilst in charge of a down goods. 53807 could be recognised immediately from all the other S & D 7Fs because when she was fitted with one of the smaller G9AS boilers, it was found that her smokebox saddle was in too poor condition to take the usual 'distance piece' to accommodate the smaller diameter of the new boiler. So she was given a new one-piece smokebox saddle. As a result 53807 was the only S & D 7F to have a small boiler, one-piece smokebox saddle, and the ejector gear on the *left* hand side of the smokebox. (Being a left-hand drive engine.)

14th May, 1955

35. With a westerly gale snatching savagely at her exhaust and sending it streaming away to the east, No. 53810 plods slowly uphill out of Chilcompton Tunnel with a heavy down goods.

9th April, 1955

36. The last of the S & D 7Fs to retain a large boiler, No. 53806, being driven by Ted Smith, climbs towards Chilcompton rock cutting with the 12.35 p.m. Bath — Evercreech Junction goods. A 'Jinty' tank is giving assistance in the rear.

16th April, 1955

37. 10 a.m. activity on a winter's morning. Ex-L.M.S. 2MT 2-6-0 No. 46494 sets off for Bristol with a local, whilst on the right Stanier 'Black Five' No. 45440 is ready to leave, as soon as the line becomes clear, with the 9.55 a.m. (9.05 a.m. ex-Bristol) down semi-fast to Bournemouth. Normally the S & D train would leave before the Bristol local, but on this occasion the position was reversed due to the late arrival of 45440's train from Bristol.

19th February, 1955

BATH, GREEN PARK, STATION

38.
August Bank Holiday Monday.
Amongst several extra trains being run from the Midlands down to Bournemouth, was a half-day excursion from Birmingham. 2P No. 40509 and B.R. class 5 No. 73073 were waiting to take over this excursion at Bath for the run down to Bournemouth, when word came through that the train was packed out, with many people having to stand. So, as can be seen in this picture, hurried arrangements were made for the two engines to collect an extra coach, ready for adding to the train as soon as it ran in. Something virtually unheard of nowadays in the 'Eighties, and certainly 'not on' with an HST! But life was different and more restful in the 'Fifties.

1st August, 1955

INTERESTING
BATH DEPARTURES

In 1955, two Summer Saturday trains from the Midlands which often had 'vintage' motive power for their run over the S & D down to Bournemouth were the 9.15 a.m. ex-Birmingham and the 7.35 a.m. ex-Nottingham. Their departures from Bath came close together, the Birmingham leaving at 12 noon, with the Nottingham following shortly afterwards at 12.24 p.m.

39. 2P No. 40700 and S & D 7F 2-8-0 No. 53804, after coupling on to the 9.15 a.m. (SO) Birmingham to Bournemouth, stand impatiently at the head of their train, waiting for the road.

10th September, 1955

40. (Below) Two S & D engines, 4F 0-6-0 No. 44559 and 7F 2-8-0 No. 53807, having taken over at Bath the 7.35 a.m. (SO) from Nottingham, set off past the old Midland shed on the run down to Bournemouth. Note the mechanical catcher arm already extended on the 7F to pick up the tablet at Bath Junction for the single line section out to Midford.

3rd September, 1955

BATH JUNCTION

For the first half-mile from Bath, Green Park, station, S & D trains ran over the Midland line. Then at Bath Junction they turned south on to their own track — which was single as far as Midford — and started to climb immediately at 1 in 50 through a long sweeping curve towards the south east.

41. Signalman Fred Davis on duty in Bath Junction Box. Just swinging south on to the S & D is the 9.15 a.m. (SO) Birmingham to Bournemouth.

27th August, 1955

42.
All down trains, as they passed the Junction Box, had to collect the tablet for the single-line section out to Midford. Nearly all engines that worked regularly over the S & D were fitted with a mechanical tablet catcher — but not elderly Johnson 0-4-4T. No. 58072, on temporary loan to Bath shed from Highbridge, which was working the 6.05 p.m. Bath — Binegar local. So the tablet had to be picked up by hand. This was done by means of the 'big pouch' — a normal tablet satchel attached to a large metal hoop which the signalman is holding up for driver Vic Hunt to collect by thrusting his arm through the hoop.

26th April, 1955

43. (Right) B.R. Standard Class 5 No. 73050 leaves the S & D single line and drifts in over Bath Junction with the up "Pines" relief.

23rd April, 1955

44. (Below) Ex-Midland 2P No. 40509 comes past the Junction Box with the 1.10 p.m. down stopping train to Templecombe. The happy person on the footplate is the well-known S.L.S. personality, W. A. Camwell.

23rd July, 1955

MIDFORD SIGNAL BOX
— and some of Midford's signals

45. In the 'Fifties, signal boxes on the Somerset and Dorset were invariably kept neat and tidy – but Midford Box stood out from all the others. Not only was it always absolutely immaculate, but it positively gleamed! The Midford signalmen responsible for this were Harry Wiltshire and Percy Savage, two dedicated railwaymen who took tremendous pride in keeping their Box second to none. Percy is the signalman on duty in this picture.
2nd April, 1955

46.
'Caught in the very act!' A picture taken at the precise moment when the mechanical catcher of 2P No. 40697 – in charge of an up train – is snatching from the line-side apparatus, the tablet for the single-line section into Bath Junction. On the left is Midford's neat Down Starter, an upper quadrant arm on a wooden post, destined in later years to be replaced by a modern Western Region type lower quadrant signal. Between the Down Starter and the engine can be seen the line-side apparatus for collecting the tablets from down trains.
2nd April, 1955

47. 7F No. 53800, hauling the 8.55 a.m. down goods, has just left the single-line section from Bath Junction — which ended two thirds of the way over Midford viaduct — and is starting the climb away from Midford on a cold morning in early February. On the left is another of Midford's attractive signals — the Up Inner Home.

12th February, 1955

48. The 3.15 p.m. down stopping train from Bath to Templecombe, drawn by 4F No. 44417, passes by the Midford Up Outer Home signal. Beneath the Outer Home arm is the 'Calling On' signal for the Inner Home.

30th May, 1955

49. 2P No. 40698 and S.R. Pacific No. 34107 "Blandford Forum", in charge of the 7.35 a.m. (SO) Nottingham to Bournemouth, pass beneath Midford's tall, graceful Down Advance Starter. Sadly, this was another of Midford's attractive signals which would be felled and replaced by a much shorter, common-place Western type soon after the Western Region had gained control of the Somerset & Dorset in 1958.

13th August, 1955

50. The up "Pines Express", drawn by 2P No. 40563 and S.R. Pacific No. 34043 "Combe Martin", has just passed underneath the ex-Great Western line from Witham to Yatton, and is running past Shepton Mallet's spacious goods yard. Being a summer Saturday, the "Pines" was not booked to stop at Shepton Mallet, and both engines are working hard to take full advantage of the brief 'dip' down to Charlton Road viaduct, before tackling the final three miles of 1 in 50 up to Masbury Summit.

23rd July, 1955

51. S & D 7F 2-8-0 No. 53808, in charge of the 4.05 p.m. down coal train from Midsomer Norton, arrives at Shepton Mallet at 4.10 p.m.! As her train was ready early, the 7F had been allowed to set off from Midsomer Norton almost 40 minutes ahead of time, but had to be shunted at Shepton Mallet to allow the 3.15 p.m. down stopping train from Bath to overtake her. Actually this practice of allowing a freight to set off as soon as the train was ready — of course always on the basis that this would not hold up any passenger service — was not uncommon on the S & D.

12th March, 1955

52. Another of the S & D 7Fs, No. 53802, after setting off from Shepton Mallet with the 4.15 p.m. up stopping train from Templecombe to Bath, has just passed over Charlton Road viaduct and is starting the climb up to Masbury Summit. Something seems to have gone a little adrift with the headlamp code! The S & D had its own headlamp code — one lamp under the chimney and one over the left hand buffer for passenger trains, and one lamp under the chimney and one over the right hand buffer for freight trains. The 317-yard long Charlton Road viaduct had 27 arches and was built on a curve. It also had the intriguing feature that halfway across, the gradient changed from 1 in 55 down to 1 in 55 up.

3rd September, 1955

53.

Except on Saturdays during the summer service, the up "Pines Express" was scheduled to make a brief stop at Shepton Mallet, arriving at 11.18 a.m. and departing one minute later at 11.19 a.m. On Easter Saturday, due to an unbalanced locomotive working, the train was hauled by two 4-6-0s, Stanier 'Black Five' No. 45440 and B.R. standard class 5 No. 73051. After their brief call, they are seen getting their train under way again for the continuation of the run up to Bath.

9th April, 1955

54. 2P No. 40564 and B.R. standard class 5 No. 73051 have just arrived at Evercreech Junction with the down "Pines Express", where the 2P is about to come off after assisting over the Mendips, whilst the class 5 will be taking water. Running in on the up line is B.R. standard class 4 2-6-0 No. 76026 with empty coaching stock from Templecombe.

9th April, 1955

APRIL SATURDAYS AT
EVERCREECH JUNCTION

55.
Fireman Reg Burt has just finished topping up the water supply of Johnson 0-4-4T. No. 58086 which would be setting off shortly with the 4.48 p.m. branch line train from Evercreech Junction over to Highbridge.

2nd April, 1955

56. 2P No. 40634 starts to get under way from the Junction with the 4.15 p.m. up stopping train from Templecombe to Bath. Standing in the middle road is Johnson 0-4-4T. No. 58086 with the stock to form the 4.48 p.m. branch line train for Highbridge. As soon as the 2P and her train have departed, 58086 will draw her train forward and then set back into the up platform.

16th April, 1955

57. Faced immediately with the commencement of the 8-mile climb up to Masbury Summit — and with no banking assistance — 7F No. 53802 makes a rousing start from Evercreech Junction Up yard with the 6.40 p.m. (SO) goods to Bath. Fireman Danny Levi looks out happily here, but he would soon be having to work very hard!

16th April, 1955

WYKE CHAMPFLOWER

After a two-mile run south from Evercreech Junction, the S & D curved sharply round to the south-east, to skirt the little village of Wyke Champflower. Scenically, this was a delightful spot, the line being bordered on both sides by beautiful trees. However, from the operating angle, it wasn't so attractive, for after a virtually straight run of two miles from Evercreech Junction, southbound trains would just be getting into their stride when drivers would have to ease off for the speed restriction of 45 m.p.h. through the Wyke curves.

58. (Left) The 3.15 p.m. down local from Bath draws near to Wyke Champflower, hauled by 2P No. 40696. The open wagon next to the engine was carrying urgently needed locomotive spares from Bath down to Templecombe shed.
3rd September, 1955

59. (Below) S & D 4F No. 44560 and B.R. class 5 No. 73052 coming up through the trees at Wyke Champflower with the 2.45 p.m. (SO) Bournemouth to Bristol.
3rd September, 1955

COLE

Cole is of considerable historical railway interest, for it was just north of here, in 1862, that the Somerset Central Railway, extending south-east from Glastonbury, met the Dorset Central Railway coming north from Templecombe. In the same year the two companies amalgamated to form the Somerset and Dorset Railway.

60. Johnson 0-4-4T. No. 58086 pauses briefly at Cole with a Templecombe–Highbridge local. Cole station was built by the Dorset Central Railway. This company's style of architecture for station buildings differed from that used by the Somerset Central Railway. In this picture, the north end of the building on the down platform shows the high gables and tall chimneys favoured by the Dorset Central Railway.

16th July, 1955

HORSINGTON

61. The 9.15 a.m. (SO) Birmingham to Bournemouth nears Horsington, half a mile north of Templecombe, hauled by an unusual combination of B.R. standard locomotives – class 4 2-6-0 No. 76010 and class 5 4-6-0 No. 73074.

16th July, 1955

62. B.R. class 5 No. 73073 sweeps up the sharp rise to No. 2 Junction with the 9.25 a.m. (SO) Bournemouth to Manchester. Templecombe engine shed can be seen in the distance on the left hand side.

16th July, 1955

TEMPLECOMBE

Somerset and Dorset trains scheduled to call at Templecombe, used the outer face of the up platform of the Southern station, which they reached by running up the spur from S & D No. 2 Junction. The procedure for carrying out this manoeuvre was most intriguing, and is set out between pictures 173 and 174 in my book "The Somerset and Dorset – An English Cross-Country Railway".*

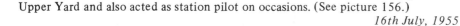

63. S & D 4F No. 44557, in charge of the 11.40 a.m. (SO) Bournemouth to Sheffield, about to pass Templecombe shed and then begin the short, sharp climb up to No. 2 Junction. On the left is ex-S.R. Z class 0-8-0T. No. 30953 which shunted Templecombe Upper Yard and also acted as station pilot on occasions. (See picture 156.)

16th July, 1955

64. Three 2P 4-4-0s, Nos. 40568, 40563 and 40569 standing outside Templecombe shed. A 3F 0-6-0, No. 43419, may just be discerned resting inside the shed. Templecombe's old wooden shed was replaced by this brick-built structure in 1950.

16th July, 1955

*Published by the
Oxford Publishing Company.

65. After calling at the Southern station – known as Templecombe Upper – S & D 7F No. 53807 and her train, the 7.43 a.m. (SO) Birmingham to Bournemouth, are being drawn out backwards down the spur to No. 2 Junction. In the foreground is the S & D main line – down which the 7F and her train would soon be travelling – which was now single for the next 16 miles as far as Blandford Forum. The small engine on the right hand side of this picture is ex-S.R. G6 class 0-6-0T. No. 30274, returning to shed after being on station pilot duties.

16th July, 1955

66. Our friend Johnson 0-4-4T. No. 58086 again. This time she is approaching Templecombe No. 2 Junction with the 9.45 a.m. local from Highbridge, and the road is set for her to run up the spur into Templecombe Upper station. The line on the right led to Templecombe Lower Yard and the engine shed. Note the attractive signals in both this picture and the one above.

16th July, 1955

67. One of the S & D's new acquisitions, B.R. standard class 4 4-6-0 No. 75071.
30th September, 1956

1956

At the beginning of June Bath M.P.D. was allocated three B.R. standard class 4 4-6-0s, Nos. 75071, 75072 and 75073 – a most welcome addition, arriving, as they did, just prior to the start of the busy summer service.

The year also saw a change in shedmaster at Bath. Mr. Webb, who had not been enjoying good health for some time, was transferred to a different appointment. The new shedmaster was Mr. Harold Morris, who had come from the mechanical side at Bristol. A thoroughly practical railwayman, with long experience on the 'running' side, Harold Morris proved an outstanding shedmaster. As it turned out, he was to be Bath's last shedmaster, for he still held the appointment when the Somerset and Dorset was closed in March 1966.

For several Sundays in the late autumn there was much activity – and not a little excitement – on the line between Binegar and Shepton Mallet where the British Transport Commission Film Unit was making an instructional film on "Emergency single-line working". This location on the Somerset and Dorset had been chosen for making the film because, after the end of the summer service, no trains ran on Sundays between Bath and Evercreech Junction, and so the Film Unit was able to have complete occupation of the line. Watching professional film-makers at work was most entertaining. The S & D staff taking part in the film were obviously enjoying themselves – and a good time was had by all!

68.
Bath's new shedmaster, Mr. Harold Morris. A deservedly popular man with the staff, Harold Morris ran Bath motive power depot with distinction for ten years, until the sad closure of the Somerset and Dorset in 1966.

69. Ready for the winter. Each winter one of Bath's 'Jinty' 0-6-0 tanks would be taken off shunting duties and made ready to act as 'snow-plough engine' should the S & D become engulfed in snow. Preparation entailed the fitting of ploughs front and rear, but before these could be attached, the engine's buffers had to be removed. 'Snow-plough engine' for the winter of 1955/56 was No. 47557.
25th February, 1956.

70. Early in February, Somerset lay under a blanket of snow, and high up on the Mendips the S & D was held in the grip of winter. On a bitterly cold morning at the beginning of February, S & D 7F 2-8-0 No. 53807 comes storming up the final few yards to Masbury Summit, 811 feet above sea level, with the 10.45 a.m. down coal train from Midsomer Norton.

4th February, 1956

WINTER COMES TO THE SOMERSET AND DORSET

71. In the 6-mile climb from Midsomer Norton, the 7F had been assisted in the rear by a 'Jinty' tank, which is seen here dropping off at the summit. The banker would now return direct to Binegar, 'wrong line', a procedure made possible by the 'Jinty' having picked up a 'bank engine key' from the lineside apparatus on her outward run through Binegar a few minutes earlier at the rear of the train.

4th February, 1956

72. Two of the S & D's new acquisitions, B.R. standard class 4 4-6-0s Nos. 75072 and 75073 set off from Evercreech Junction with the 2.45 p.m. (SO) Bournemouth to Bristol. The crew of 75072 are driver Arthur Sellman and fireman Ralph Holden with driver Cecil Waldron in charge of 75073. (Unfortunately my notes, made at the time of taking the picture, failed to record the name of 75073's fireman.)

30th June, 1956

THE SOMERSET AND DORSET RECEIVES ITS FIRST ALLOCATION OF B.R. STANDARD CLASS 4 4-6-0s

In June, B.R. standard class 4 4-6-0s appeared on the S & D scene for the first time. Three of the class, Nos. 75070, 75071 and 75072 were scheduled for transfer from Exmouth Junction M.P.D. to Bath; in the event however, 75070 did not come to the S & D, being replaced by 75073.

73.
(Above) No. 75071, piloting S.R. Pacific No. 34107 "Blandford Forum", appears round the bend heading south from Midford with the 7.35 a.m. (SO) Nottingham to Bournemouth. Standing on the left are 2P No. 40634 and S.R. Pacific No. 34041 "Wilton", in charge of the 10.05 a.m. (SO) Bournemouth to Cleethorpes, waiting for the single-line section into Bath Junction to become clear.
4th August, 1956

74.
(Left) No. 75073, assisted by ex-S & D 4F No. 44557, draws near to Wellow in the late afternoon with the 10.38 a.m. (SO) Manchester to Bournemouth.
4th August, 1956

75. '993' – from Birmingham, New Street – drawn by 2P No. 40696 and 'Black Five' No. 44917, passing through Midsomer Norton station. This train was due off Bath at 11.47 a.m. There was a five minute stop (12.35 – 12.40) at Shepton Mallet for water – where the 2P came off – and the excursion then ran non-stop to Poole (arr. 1.53, dep. 1.56). Arrival time at Bournemouth West was 2.08 p.m. The return run to Birmingham left Bournemouth at 7.30 p.m.

20th May, 1956

WHIT SUNDAY EXCURSIONS OVER THE S & D DOWN TO BOURNEMOUTH

In the 1950s Bournemouth was a popular destination for excursion trains run by B.R. on Bank Holidays. On Whit Sunday 1956 – a glorious summer's day – the three half-day excursions which ran to Bournemouth over the S & D, came from Bristol, Birmingham and Cheltenham.

77. (Right) '997' – from Cheltenham – hauled by ex-Midland 2P No. 40509 and B.R. class 5 No. 73047, climbing towards Chilcompton Tunnel. Bath had been left at 11.10 a.m. and, like the other two excursions, there was a five minute stop (11.58 – 12.03) at Shepton Mallet to detach the 2P and for the class 5 to take water. The train then ran non-stop to Poole (1.18 – 1.20) and arrived at Bournemouth West at 1.28 p.m. The return run to Cheltenham in the evening left Bournemouth at 8.10 p.m.

20th May, 1956

76. 'M994' – the excursion from Bristol – in the charge of 2P No. 40700 and B.R. class 5 No. 73050, draws near to Binegar. This train left Bath at 10.10 a.m. and picked up passengers on the S & D at Radstock (10.30), Midsomer Norton (10.38), Shepton Mallet (11.02 – 11.07) – where the class 5 took water and the 2P came off – and Wincanton (11.27). Poole was reached at 12.28 and Bournemouth West at 12.40 p.m. The return run left Bournemouth at 7.05 p.m.

20th May, 1956

78. 2P No. 40634 and B.R. class 5 No. 73050 climbing vigorously uphill out of Chilcompton Tunnel with the down "Pines Express".

7th August, 1956

"THE PINES EXPRESS"
— The pride of the S & D

79.
A close-up of the crew of the class 5, driver Bert Brewer — leaning out of the cab window — and fireman Alan Northover.

80.
— And the crew of the 2P shortly before leaving Bath — driver Pat Evans (right) and fireman Fred Gray.

7th August, 1956

81.
The normal motive power for "The Pines Express" was a class 5, with a Templecombe 2P giving assistance over the Mendips between Evercreech Junction and Bath. Occasionally however — as on this Saturday the week before Whitsun — the up "Pines" would run in one part, whilst the down train in the afternoon would be in two parts. Two class 5s would then be put on the up train in the morning so that there would be a class 5 for each of the down trains in the afternoon. In this picture B.R. class 5s Nos. 73050 and 73047 are running in past the entrance to Bath sheds with the up "Pines Express". The driver of 73050 was Donald Beale.
12th May, 1956

82. The very difficult nature of the S & D route produced many outstanding enginemen, but none finer than Donald Beale whose superb artistry in the handling of a steam locomotive has made him a legend in his life time. I took this picture of Donald at Evercreech Junction when he had 73050 on the down "Pines Express" one Saturday in late October.
27th October, 1956

83. Driver Arthur Clist and his mate, passed fireman 'Bill' Bailey, pose for me in front of their class 5, No. 73052, after bringing in the up "Pines" from Bournemouth. Arthur Clist, an expert engineman, was one of the most genial and popular drivers on the S & D, and at the time of his retirement in 1955, was senior driver of "The Pines Express". (This picture should really have come in '1955', but I wanted to include Arthur with his Branksome colleagues Bert Brewer and Donald Beale.)

84. On a warm, still afternoon in late spring, the 4.37 p.m. down local, hauled by 2P No. 40697, heads south through the beautiful countryside around Wellow.
12th May, 1956

WELLOW

— One of several attractive small villages which used to be served by the Somerset and Dorset.

85. (Below) In sharp contrast to the picture above, the weather on the third Saturday in July was miserable. The morning had started off overcast and as the day wore on, conditions steadily deteriorated. This is one of the few pictures I took that day. In the light drizzle which had set in by mid afternoon, ex-Midland 2P No. 40509 and B.R. class 5 No. 73047 pass Wellow with the 2.45 p.m. (SO) Bournemouth to Bristol. In the background is the tower of St. Julian's church, Wellow, which dates from the 14th century.
21st July, 1956

86. 4F No. 44560 sweeps through the curves west of Wellow with the 4.26 p.m. down semi-fast from Bath.

The Somerset and Dorset Railway and the Wellow Brook were never far apart as they wended their way through the Midford and Wellow valleys. The fishing may have been private, but anyone was free to enjoy the entrancing sight of an S & D train gliding through the lovely Somerset countryside around Wellow. *12th May, 1956*

THE S & D 7F 2-8-0s

By 1956 all five of the large-boilered engines built by Robert Stephenson & Co. in 1925 had been re-boilered. So now the entire class of eleven engines had the smaller G9AS type boiler of 4 ft. 9^1/$_8$ in. diameter.

87. S & D 7F No. 53810, a re-boilered version of the Stephenson-built engines of 1925. Note the 'distance-piece' inserted in the smokebox saddle to accommodate the smaller diameter of the G9AS type boiler. It may be of interest to compare this near-side view of 53810 with the off-side picture 53807 in plate 34.

14th October, 1956

88. No. 53804, one of the original batch built at Derby in 1914, comes thundering up the 1 in 50 towards Combe Down Tunnel with the 12.35 p.m. down goods from Bath to Evercreech Junction.

22nd May, 1956

89. No. 53806 bursts out of Devonshire Tunnel into the sunshine of Lyncombe Vale during her climb up the 1 in 50 bank out of Bath with the 8.55 a.m. down goods.

21st April, 1956

90.
Except on summer Saturdays, it was rare to see an S & D 7F on a passenger train. In this instance No. 53805 had been commandeered at short notice to work the 4.37 p.m. down stopping train — seen here approaching Midsomer Norton — when the 2P booked for the turn, failed just before coming off shed. Lacking the necessary equipment to steam heat the train, 05 can't have been very popular with her passengers on this decidedly chilly day in early spring!

2nd April, 1956

CHILCOMPTON TUNNEL

This short tunnel — it was only 66 yards long — came between Midsomer Norton and Chilcompton in the climb up the northern slopes of the Mendips.

93. (Opposite page, top)
B.R. class 5 No. 73047, with her load of 8 coaches, comes toiling up the long stretch of 1 in 53 towards the deep cutting leading to the tunnel. The train was a relief to the down "Pines Express" — 10.30 a.m. Liverpool, Lime Street to Bournemouth West — and being less than 270 tons the class 5 was not entitled to an assisting engine for the climb over the Mendips. (Hard luck on the fireman on a hot day like this!)
19th May, 1956

91. In the late afternoon of a warm, sunny Saturday in May, the 5.00 p.m. down goods from Bath to Evercreech Junction emerges, hauled by S & D 7F No. 53804.
19th May, 1956

92. The down "Pines Express" about to pass through the tunnel. The engines are 4F No. 44096 and B.R. class 5 No. 73051.
2nd April, 1956

94. A pair of 2Ps, Nos. 40700 and 40564, sweep down the bank towards the tunnel with the 4.15 p.m. up stopping train from Templecombe to Bath. 40700 had assisted a down train over the Mendips earlier in the day and was coupled ahead of 40564 for the run back to Bath to save having to find a separate light engine path for her.

19th May, 1956

WINSOR HILL TUNNEL

In the ascent of the southern slopes of the Mendips, the Somerset and Dorset passed through Winsor Hill Tunnel, situated some 2 miles north of Shepton Mallet, as the line climbed at 1 in 50 towards Masbury Summit. The up and down lines passed through separate bores.

The extension of the Somerset and Dorset from Evercreech Junction up to Bath, completed in 1874, was originally constructed as a single line. When the Shepton Mallet – Binegar section was doubled in 1892, it was decided to deviate a short distance to the west at Winsor Hill so that the tunnel for the new (up) line could be 110 yards shorter than the original tunnel. The length of the old tunnel, used by the down line, was 242 yards, whereas the new tunnel was only 132 yards long.

95. Travelling at high speed, 2P No. 40568 and 'Black Five' No. 44917 leave Winsor Hill Tunnel on their rapid descent of the southern slopes of the Mendips with the down "Pines Express".

The catch points on the up line were strategically placed to deal with any break-aways from goods trains toiling up the long stretch of 1 in 50.
31st March, 1956

96. In sharp contrast to the picture above, S & D 7F 2-8-0 No. 53803 emerged from the tunnel at a very sedate pace as, with complete control over her train, she coasted down the long bank in charge of the 12.35 p.m. Bath – Evercreech Junction goods.
21st April, 1956

97. S & D 7F 2-8-0 No. 53810 toils up the long stretch of 1 in 50 towards Winsor Hill Tunnel with a heavy north-bound goods. Giving hearty banking assistance in the rear is 3F 0-6-0 No. 43194 — an old S & D stalwart, having been built for the line by the Midland Railway at Derby in 1896.

14th October, 1956

98. A distant view from the top of Winsor Hill of a north-bound evening goods climbing up the southern slopes of the Mendips towards the tunnel.
29th September, 1956

THE MAKING OF THE FILM "EMERGENCY SINGLE-LINE WORKING"

In 1956 British Railways decided to produce, for staff training, an instructional film on Emergency Single-line Working. Because, after the end of the summer service, no trains ran on Sundays between Bath and Evercreech Junction, the Somerset and Dorset line was selected for the making of the film, and this took place on Sundays in September and October.

As the film was intended for showing throughout B.R., considerable pains were taken to try and prevent it from being identified with any particular Region. Shepton Mallet and Binegar, the two stations which appeared in the film, had their names changed to "Averton Hammer" and "Boiland" respectively. For passenger train sequences, the engines used were B.R. standard class 4 and class 5 4-6-0s — types which could have been seen anywhere on B.R. However, when it came to filming the goods train scenes, the cat was well and truly let out of the bag, for the engine used was one of the highly individual S & D 7F 2-8-0s!

99. Binegar becomes "Boiland".
30th September, 1956

100. B.R. class 4 4-6-0 No. 75071 prepares to do her fourth run in to Binegar for a 'passenger arrival' scene. I was roped in to be one of the passengers 'alighting at Boiland'. It was all great fun — we must have 'alighted at Boiland' at least half a dozen times — but sadly this particular sequence ended up on the cutting room floor!

30th September, 1956

101. The director of the B.T.C. Film Unit, Mr. Fairbairn (arm raised), gives some last-minute instructions to the driver before the filming of a 'setting-back' sequence, whilst Inspector Henman supports a member of the camera crew, perched rather precariously at the back of the tender. (On the first 'take', the engine was unfortunately in forward gear!)

14th October, 1956

102. S & D 7F No. 53810 prepares to set off, wrong road, from 'Boiland' with a down goods. Mr. Fairbairn is having a final word with the engine crew before departure.

14th October, 1956

103. Coming up to Masbury Summit, wrong road. Note that not only was the engine one of the highly individual S & D 7F 2-8-0s, but it also carried the S & D's own headlamp code!

14th October, 1956

104. The up "Pines Express", hauled by 2P No. 40568 and 'Black Five' No. 44917, coming in over the facing crossover by the Station Box so as to run in to the platform on the south side of Green Park station. The "Pines" always used this platform as it was slightly longer than the one on the north side. (Even so, it could only accommodate nine coaches and an engine).

2nd April, 1956

'MORNING'

BATH, GREEN PARK, STATION

105. 2P No. 40634 (built at Derby for the S & D.J.R. in 1928) and S.R. Pacific No. 34041 "Wilton" standing in Bath station after arriving with the up "Pines Express". With twelve on, and two engines, quite a bit of the 'tail' of the "Pines" would be standing beyond the end of the platform, out on the river bridge! The crew of the 2P are passed fireman Trevor Netley and fireman Mike Fudge.

25th August, 1956

106. A busy time at Bath, Green Park. In the right hand (south) platform, ex-L.M.S. class 2MT 2-6-0 No. 46400 has just coupled on to the 3.35 p.m. from Bournemouth — the 'Up Mail' — which she will take out at 7.03 p.m. for the run up to Mangotsfield. After connecting there with the north-bound mail, the 2-6-0 would then take her train down the bank into Bristol, Temple Meads. In the north platform B.R. class 4 2-6-0 No. 76028 stands at the head of the 6.02 p.m. Bristol, Temple Meads to Bournemouth West, with which she will set off at 7.05 p.m. — two minutes after the departure of the 'Up Mail'. Standing in the middle road, on carriage shunting duties, is 2P No. 40569.

30th May, 1956

'EVENING'

107. One evening in early February the 'Up Mail' arrived in Bath hauled, most unusually, by one of the attractive ex-L & S.W.R. T9 4-4-0s, No. 30706. The appearance of a T9 on the S & D was a rare occurrence. On this occasion, Bournemouth Central M.P.D. had turned out 30706 at short notice to replace the booked engine, a B.R. standard class 4, which had failed.

2nd February, 1956

108. "It's Quicker by Train" — and also much more 'serene and delightful' if travelling by the S & D!

5th May, 1957

(For the record, 5th May was a Sunday. 76007 is crossing over the Lower Bristol Road, Bath, in the early morning on her way, light engine, to some engineering work south of Midsomer Norton.)

1957

1957 proved to be a rather 'uneventful' year for the Somerset and Dorset; apart from the usual excitement of summer Saturdays, life on the S & D went on much as usual. Notwithstanding Bath M.P.D.'s acquisition of three B.R. standard class 4 4-6-0s, use still had to be made of the S & D 7F 2-8-0s for hauling passenger trains on Saturdays at the height of the summer service. On the branch, the Johnson 3F 0-6-0s continued to put in useful work, but sadly, by 1957, only one Johnson 1P 0-4-4T., No. 58086, remained on the Somerset and Dorset, the Ivatt 2-6-2Ts having taken over the working of the majority of the Highbridge — Templecombe passenger trains.

109. The S & D's last Johnson 0-4-4T., No. 58086, on Highbridge shed. (There were only five of the class left in the whole of the country.)

18th August, 1957

110.   Ivatt 2-6-2T. No. 41304 heading north from Cole with the 3.05 p.m. (SO) Templecombe — Evercreech Junction local.
7th September, 1957

As the Johnson 0-4-4 tanks faded from the S & D scene, the working of the Highbridge — Templecombe passenger service was taken over by Johnson 3F 0-6-0s and Ivatt 2-6-2Ts.

111.   The 2.20 p.m. Highbridge — Templecombe local, hauled by Johnson 3F 0-6-0 No. 43194, passing over Cole viaduct. 43194 was built for the line by the Midland Railway Co. at their Derby Works in 1896. Her original S & D.J.R. number was 62.

7th September, 1957

B.R. CLASS 4 2-6-0s ON THE S & D

No B.R. standard class 4 2-6-0s were ever allocated to an S & D depot, but Eastleigh regularly rostered this type for work over the S & D from Bournemouth up to Bath and back.

112. B.R. standard class 4 2-6-0 No. 76019, with driver Arthur King in charge, passing Midford Up Distant signal with the 1.10 p.m. from Bournemouth West.
20th April, 1957

113. 2P No. 40698 and B.R. class 4 2-6-0 No. 76012 appear from round a bend in the Midford Valley as they head north with the 1.08 p.m. (SO) Bournemouth West to Bristol, Temple Meads.
13th July, 1957

114. Easter was late in 1957. A Bank Holiday Monday excursion from Birmingham to Bournemouth sets off from Bath hauled by two B.R. standard 4-6-0s, class 4 No. 75071 and class 5 No. 73047.

22nd April, 1957

B.R. CLASS 4 4-6-0s ON THE S & D

Several standard class 4 4-6-0s were allocated to Bath M.P.D., and later also to Templecombe M.P.D.

115. A pair of Bath's class 4s, Nos. 75071 and 75073, dart out of Chilcompton Tunnel during their swift descent of the northern slopes of the Mendips with the 2.45p.m. (SO) Bournemouth to Bristol.

29th June, 1957

116.
The down "Pines Express", hauled by 2P No. 40634 and B.R. class 5 No. 73050, running through the Midford Valley near Twinhoe on a cold but sunny winter's afternoon in early February. Driver Donald Beale was in charge on the class 5, with Peter Smith as his fireman.
9th February, 1957

B.R. CLASS 5 4-6-0s ON THE S & D

From 1954 onwards, the S & D had an allocation of B.R. standard class 5 4-6-0s, with additional engines of this class being temporarily transferred to the line for use during the Summer service. All the class 5s were shedded at Bath.

118.
(Right) Another of the S & D's B.R. class 5s, No. 73051, assisted by 2P No. 40696, gets away from the Midsomer Norton stop with the August Bank Holiday half-day excursion from Bath to Bournemouth. This train, which left Bath at 11.00 a.m., picked up passengers at most of the stations down the line as far south as Cole. Bournemouth arrival time was 1.45 p.m.

5th August, 1957

119. (Below) Five minutes after the excursion had departed southwards, the up "Pines Express" came sweeping downhill round the curve, hauled by 2P No. 40569 and B.R. class 5 No. 73116, on loan to Bath M.P.D. from Nine Elms M.P.D. for the duration of the summer service. *5th August, 1957*

117.
(Left) The up "Pines Express" coming past Wellow on Easter Saturday, hauled by class 5s Nos. 73050 and 73052. It was unusual to have two class 5s on the "Pines" and this only occurred when the "Pines Express" became unbalanced as used to happen sometimes at Easter and Whitsun. When the up "Pines" ran as one train — as on this occasion — but the down was in two parts, two class 5s would bring the up "Pines" from Bournemouth to Bath in the morning, and in the afternoon each would return to Bournemouth with a part of the down "Pines".

20th April, 1957

THE S & D 7F 2-8-0s ON PASSENGER WORK

Notwithstanding Bath shed's acquisition of three B.R. standard class 4 4-6-0s, use still had to be made of the S & D 7Fs for hauling passenger trains on Saturdays at the height of the summer service.

120. 2P No. 40696 and 7F No. 53803, hauling the 10.35 a.m. (SO) Bournemouth West to Manchester, Victoria, come round the sharp curve leading away from Evercreech Junction North Box in very determined manner at the start of their 8-mile climb up to Masbury Summit. The crew of the 2P are driver Fred Wotley and fireman White, and driver Donald Beale and fireman Peter Smith are on the 7F.

3rd August, 1957

121.
After taking the picture above, I made a dash for my car and just managed to beat the train to Masbury, to get this further picture of my friends topping the summit in fine style. (Peter Smith had obviously been hard at work for the 7F to be blowing off after her 8-mile climb!)

3rd August, 1957

122. The first Saturday in August — the busiest day of the year for the S & D — had been a glorious summer's day. In the late afternoon, towards the end of a very happy day's photography, I 'chased' S & D 7F No. 53810 and B.R. class 4 No. 75072, with the 10.28 a.m. (SO) Manchester, London Road, to Bournemouth West, from Midsomer Norton up to Masbury, and got this final picture of them, bathed in evening sunshine, as they came steadily up to the Summit.

3rd August, 1957

An interesting feature of the 7F diagrams for passenger work on summer Saturdays in 1957, was the greater use made of these 2-8-0 locomotives as assisting engines rather than train engines. This was a sensible move for, in the main, it limited their running to between Evercreech Junction and Bath, and whereas the 7Fs were excellent engines for assisting heavy expresses over the Mendips, the less high speed running they had to do, the better for both engine and footplate crew!

123.

After being held at Midford's Up Outer Home signal, waiting for the single line section into Bath Junction to become clear, S & D 7F No. 53805 and B.R. class 5 No. 73087, in charge of the 8.40 a.m. (SO) Bournemouth West to Bradford, Forster Square, get away smartly for the coming climb up to Combe Down Tunnel. 73087 was another of the S & D's temporary acquisitions for the summer service, being on loan from Stewarts Lane M.P.D.

10th August, 1957

124. S & D 7F No. 53800 and B.R. class 5 No. 73052 climbing south from Moorewood towards Binegar with 'W196', the 10.28 a.m. (SO) Manchester, London Road, to Bournemouth West.

31st August, 1957

THE S & D 7F 2-8-0s AS ASSISTING ENGINES ON PASSENGER TRAINS

125.
The 11.40 a.m. (SO) Bournemouth to Sheffield coming up over Prestleigh viaduct, hauled by S & D 7F No. 53801 and B.R. class 5 No. 73047.

7th September, 1957

126.
Our friend 'W196' again, this time at Masbury Summit on a very wet Saturday in late July. B.R. class 4 4-6-0 No. 75072, assisted by S & D 7F No. 53810, reaches the summit with the 10.28 a.m. (SO) Manchester to Bournemouth. The crew of the 4-6-0 – looking cheerful even in the rain! – are driver Ray Stokes and fireman Mike Fudge.

27th July, 1957

— AND THE S & D 7Fs
ON THEIR NORMAL DUTIES

127. A Sunday ballast climbing the bank out of Bath hauled by 7F No. 53805 and banked in the rear by a 4F 0-6-0 working tender-first. (The 4F had earlier worked the ballast down the Midland line from Westerleigh to Bath.)

5th May, 1957

128.
7F No. 53807 starting the climb out of Bath with the 12.35 p.m. down goods on a bright, but cold day in early November. The Midland bracket signal told drivers of in-coming trains whether they had the road to run in on the main line or the goods loop.

2nd November, 1957

LYNCOMBE VALE

The very attractive wooded section leading up to Combe Down Tunnel which came at the end of the climb out of Bath.

129. An Easter Monday Bank Holiday excursion from Bristol to Bournemouth coming up to Combe Down Tunnel hauled by B.R. class 5 No. 73051, assisted by 4F No. 44422. This is the 4F which has been preserved by the North Staffordshire Railway Society.

22nd April, 1957

130.
2P No. 40569 and S.R. "Battle of Britain" Pacific No. 34109 "Sir Trafford Leigh Mallory" leave Combe Down Tunnel with the up "Pines Express".
29th June, 1957

131. The up "Pines Express", drawn by 2P No. 40569 and B.R. class 5 No. 73047, emerges from the gloom of Combe Down Tunnel into Lyncombe Vale and the sparkling sunshine of a fresh spring day.

6th April, 1957

MIDFORD

132. The 8.00 a.m. up goods from Evercreech Junction coming across Midford viaduct hauled by S & D 7F No. 53801. The driver is working his engine hard so as to get up as much speed as possible for the climb up to, and through, Combe Down Tunnel.

4th May, 1957

133. Ex-S & D No. 44559, in charge of the 4.37 p.m. down stopping train from Bath to Templecombe, climbs away southwards up the 1 in 60 past Midford's tall, stately Down Advance Starting signal.

11th June, 1957

IN SUNSHINE —

134. The 3.20 p.m. Bath — Templecombe down stopping train, hauled by another of the ex-S & D 4Fs, No. 44557, leaves the viaduct after the stop at Midford station, seen in the distance. Note how the four-mile single-line section from Bath Junction ended near the southern end of the viaduct. The line was now double-track for the next 32 miles as far as Templecombe.

5th October, 1957

— AND IN RAIN

135.
The second Saturday in August started off wet, but the rain soon eased to a light drizzle which finally petered out about mid-morning. Before the weather had started to improve, a rare visitor to the S & D, ex-L.M.S. Caprotti class 5 No. 44744, appeared through the gloom, running towards Midford with the 8.00 a.m. (SO) Bournemouth West to Sheffield (Midland).
10th August, 1957

MIDFORD

Up trains booked to cross down trains at the southern end of the single line section between Bath Junction and Midford, were held at Midford's Up Outer Home signal. This was an interesting and most pleasant location for watching S & D trains. The signal was sited about ¼ mile south of Midford viaduct in beautiful countryside, and with the main road some distance away on the far side of the valley, there was little to disturb the serenity of this delightful spot.

136. The 2.45 p.m. (SO) Bournemouth to Bristol, hauled by two of Bath's B.R. class 4 4-6-0s Nos. 75073 and 75071, is held at Midford Up Outer Home signal, waiting for the single-line section into Bath Junction to become clear. This train was booked to run non-stop from Evercreech Junction to Bath, but she was brought to a stand at Midford due to the late-running of the 4.37 p.m. down from Bath, seen approaching headed by 4F No. 44102.

6th July, 1957

137.
S & D 7F No. 53809, running one hour *early* (!) with the 3.20 p.m. (SX) up goods from Evercreech Junction, found she had to pay the price with a long, tedious wait at Midford for the single-line into Bath Junction. Three down trains, all running to schedule, occupied in succession the single-line section before 53809 was allowed to run in with her train. About to pass by 53809 is the third of the down trains, the 5.00 p.m. Bath-Evercreech Junction goods, hauled by sister engine No. 53806.

11th June, 1957

138. The 7.18 p.m. down goods from Bath to Templecombe, bathed in late evening sunshine, passes over Wellow viaduct drawn by S & D 7F No. 53804.

22nd May, 1957

BETWEEN MIDFORD AND WELLOW

139. 2P No. 40700 running through the enchanting countryside around Twinhoe as she heads towards Wellow with the 3.20 p.m. down stopping train from Bath to Templecombe.

11th May, 1957

MAY EVENING

140. The evening of Wednesday, May 22nd, was warm and almost cloudless, so I decided I would follow the 7.18 p.m. Bath – Templecombe goods down the line as far as Masbury Summit. The train was hauled by S & D 7F No. 53804 and I was able to get several pictures of her during her journey south. On the previous page she is seen crossing over Wellow viaduct, and in this picture, taken shortly before sunset, the train is climbing towards Chilcompton rock cutting.

22nd May, 1957

CHILCOMPTON

141. The morning of Saturday, 2nd November, was also almost cloudless – but the temperature, at a shade above freezing, was vastly different from the warm summer evening when I took the picture above! On this occasion I had got up early to follow a northbound goods – the 6.05 a.m. Templecombe to Bath, seen here dropping down the bank through Chilcompton station in the charge of 7F No. 53810. On the left is my Bentley, NHY 581, 'waiting for the off'. Like her predecessor, MYD 50, she came to know the S & D so well, that there can hardly have been a road, lane or farm track, which ran beside, over or under the line, that she did not traverse at sometime or another.

2nd November, 1957

NOVEMBER MORNING

SOUTH OF SHEPTON MALLET

142. Two B.R. class 4 4-6-0s, Nos. 75072 and 75073, crossing over Prestleigh viaduct with the 2.45 p.m. (SO) Bournemouth to Bristol, during the course of their climb up the southern slopes of the Mendips.

31st August, 1957

143. 2P No. 40569 and S.R. Pacific No. 34107 "Blandford Forum", hauling the up "Pines Express", near the end of a gruelling three-mile stretch of 1 in 50, as they approach Shepton Mallet.

7th September, 1957

144. A sign of the times! — a 4-6-0 appears amongst the 2Ps in a summer Saturday line-up of assisting engines at Evercreech Junction. On this first Saturday in August the assisting engines were — 2Ps Nos. 40568 and 40564, B.R. class 4 No. 75073 and 2P No. 40696.

3rd August, 1957

145.
Evercreech Departure. After taking water, S & D 7F No. 53804 sets off over the level crossing and past the water tower at the southern end of the station, as she resumes her run down to Bournemouth with a Saturday relief from Walsall. The driver of the 7F is Archie Gunning.

27th July, 1957

THE BASON BRIDGE — TEMPLECOMBE MILK

This train ran seven days a week to connect at Templecombe with the milk train for London from the South West.

146. Perfect timing by 3F No. 43194! Just as a heavy summer thunderstorm ended and the sun came out — in she rolled to the Junction with the afternoon 'milk', to come to a stand by the column to take water. (Not that anybody else wanted any — everything was awash!)

8th June, 1957

147. The afternoon 'milk', again hauled by 3F No. 43194 and this time driven by Charlie King, comes in off the branch at Evercreech Junction. The main line to Bath can just be seen on the right, curving away sharply to the north.

7th September, 1957

148. A close-up of Driver Charlie King and fireman Keith Conibear in the cab of 43194.

COLE

Where the Somerset Central Railway joined up with the Dorset Central Railway in 1862 to become the Somerset and Dorset Railway.

149. 3F No. 43218 stands in Cole station with the 2.20 p.m. Highbridge – Templecombe local, waiting for the road. 43218 was one of the Somerset and Dorset's 'old stalwarts'; as No. 73, she had been built for the S & D.J.R. by Neilson, Reid & Co. way back in 1902.

15th June, 1957

150. Stanier 'Black Five' No. 45440 nearing Cole with the 6.57 a.m. (SO) Cleethorpes to Bournemouth. 45440 was one of the S & D's first 'Black Fives'. As 'Fifty-four forty' – and when just a few months old – she had been allocated to the Somerset and Dorset in 1938. Sadly, 1957 was destined to be her last year on the S & D.

15th June, 1957

151. B.R. class 4 4-6-0 No. 75072 passing over Cole viaduct with the 2.45 p.m. (SO) Bournemouth to Bristol on a warm, still afternoon in early September.

7th September, 1957

152. Saturday, 27th July, was not only gloomy and overcast, but also one of those days when nothing went right for the S & D. Down trains from the Midlands and the North had been arriving increasingly late at Bath, and this threw into confusion all the carefully worked out crossings with up trains on the single-line sections. And of course it had to happen on one of the busiest days of the year for the S & D. Passing through Cole on the down line — and running over half an hour late — is the 7.35 a.m. (SO) Nottingham to Bournemouth, hauled by S.R. "Battle of Britain" Pacific No. 34110 "66 Squadron". On the up line, B.R. class 5 No. 73051, after being held at Cole's Home signal with the 8-coach 12.20 p.m. Bournemouth — Birmingham relief, had been brought forward to the box so that the signalman could tell the footplate crew what was causing their protracted delay. — The engine on the preceding train wasn't steaming well, and with no assisting engine available, she was still standing in Evercreech Junction station, having a 'blow-up'.

27th July, 1957

TEMPLECOMBE

153. Activity on Templecombe shed. S & D 7F 2-8-0 No. 53800 engaged in shunting three 'dead' engines, S.R. class G6 0-6-0T. No. 30274, L.M.S. Ivatt 2-6-2T. No. 41248 and S & D.J.R. 3F 0-6-0 No. 43216. Standing on the right is M.R. 3F 0-6-0 No. 43419. The brick-built shed was erected in 1950, replacing an earlier wooden structure.
20th July, 1957

154.
The 7.35 a.m. (SO) Nottingham to Bournemouth, hauled by S.R. "West Country" Pacific No. 34108 "Wincanton", dropping down from No. 2 Junction, past S & D 7F No. 53805 standing in Templecombe Lower Yard.
20th July, 1957

155.
The 7.43 a.m. (SO) Birmingham, New Street, to Bournemouth West, hauled by B.R. class 4 4-6-0 No. 75073, passing by the engine shed and the site of the original Dorset Central Railway station at Templecombe. The old D.C.R. station buildings with typical high gables, can be seen on this side of the shed. In latter days it was used as part of the Motive Power Depot offices and stores.
20th July, 1957

156.   The 9.55 a.m. Bath — Bournemouth semi-fast, having called at Templecombe Upper (the S.R. station), is drawn out backwards and down the spur to No. 2 Junction by S.R. 'Z' class 0-8-0T. No. 30953. The train engine, S & D 7F No. 53804, remained attached at the other end throughout this movement.   *20th July, 1957*

157.   The 'Z' having been uncoupled, the 7F sets off from No. 2 Junction on the resumption of the journey down to Bournemouth. For the next 16 miles, as far as Blandford Forum, the S & D line was now single-track. The crew of the 7F are driver Harry Saunders and fireman John Cockerill.   *20th July, 1957*

1958

In 1958 there was a reshuffle of the regional boundaries and the major part of the Somerset and Dorset fell into the hands of the Western Region. At the time, few realised the fateful implications of this change, but, with hindsight, it was the death warrant for the Somerset and Dorset. Apart from Branksome, all S & D sheds were transferred to the Western Region, the new shed codes being, Bath (with sub-sheds Radstock and Highbridge) 82F, and Templecombe 82G. The S & D's last two Stanier 'Black Fives', No. 44917 and the 'old faithful', No. 45440, were handed back to the London Midland Region, and as replacements, the Western Region transferred from Bristol, two of their B.R. standard class 5s, Nos. 73019 and 73028. In May the S & D had its first taste of diesel, when two DMU-worked excursions ran over the line; and at the end of the year, sundry ex-G.W.R. engines appeared on the scene for 'clearance' tests.

158.   Midford. The up "Pines Express" hauled by 2P No. 40569 and S.R. Pacific No. 34040 "Crewkerne", 'framed' by the Down Starter and Calling Back signals. The Pacific is just about to collect the tablet for the single-line section into Bath Junction. The Western Region replaced several S & D signals with their own type, including Midford's Down Starter and the tall, stately Advance Starter. But the distinctive S & D Calling Back signals were left untouched until the death of the line in 1966.
14th June, 1958

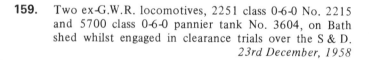

159.   Two ex-G.W.R. locomotives, 2251 class 0-6-0 No. 2215 and 5700 class 0-6-0 pannier tank No. 3604, on Bath shed whilst engaged in clearance trials over the S & D.
23rd December, 1958

THE FIRST APPEARANCE OF DIESEL MULTIPLE UNITS ON THE SOMERSET AND DORSET

Although DMU excursions ran over the line occasionally, the S & D remained a 'steam' line to the end. No regular trains were ever diesel-powered.

160. An 8-car DMU, which formed a Whit Sunday excursion from Birmingham to Bournemouth, coasts down past Midford goods yard. On the right, 'NHY 581' is poised ready to give chase up to Masbury Summit.

25th May, 1958

161.
The first DMU to run over the S & D was a 3-car unit forming an enthusiasts' special organised by the Gloucestershire Railway Society. The train is seen here climbing past Midsomer Norton station.

10th May, 1958

SUNDAY BALLAST WORKINGS

With no trains scheduled to run over the S & D between Bath and Evercreech Junction on winter Sundays, this was the ideal day of the week for ballast workings, because the engineers' department could have complete occupation of the line without disorganising any regular service.

162. In crisp winter sunshine on the first Sunday morning in January, two S & D 7F 2-8-0s lift a ballast train up the 1 in 50 bank out of Bath. The train engine is No. 53803, one of the original batch built at Derby in 1914.
5th January, 1958

163. — Whilst giving whole-hearted assistance in the rear is No. 53806, one of the five S & D 7Fs built by Robert Stephenson & Co. in 1925.

5th January, 1958

164. On the second Sunday in January, S & D 7F No. 53800 emerges from Devonshire Tunnel at the head of the train, climbing vigorously up the 1 in 50 bank through Lyncombe Vale.

12th January, 1958

165. — And banked in the rear by sister engine No. 53802.

12th January, 1958

THE FOLLOWING SUNDAY SAW A 'REPEAT PERFORMANCE'

166. On this Sunday the ballasting was taking place half a mile south of Moorewood, and for the climb up the northern slopes of the Mendips the train was banked by 4F 0-6-0 No. 44096, which came on at Radstock. In this picture the train is climbing up the long stretch of 1 in 50 towards Midsomer Norton.

12th January, 1958

167. The down "Pines Express", hauled by 2P No. 40564 and B.R. class 5 No. 73028, appears from out of the cutting, running downhill towards Midford.

7th June, 1958

CLASS 5 CHANGES

The Western Region transfer two of their B.R. standard class 5 4-6-0s, Nos. 73019 and 73028, to Bath M.P.D. to replace the S & D's last two remaining Stanier 'Black Fives', Nos. 44917 and 45440, which had been returned to the London Midland Region.

168. B.R. class 5 No. 73019 nearing Wyke Champflower with a relief from Leicester (2.06 p.m. off Bath). Note the ex-L.N.E.R. articulated stock next to the engine.

2nd August, 1958

169. The 7.18 p.m. Bath — Templecombe freight passing over Wellow viaduct, hauled by B.R. class 5 No. 73047.
31st May, 1958

B.R. CLASS 5s ON FREIGHTS

The use of the S & D's expanding stud of B.R. class 5s is extended to freight working.

170.
On a beautiful summer's evening in early July, B.R. class 5 No. 73050 draws near to Wellow with the 4.45 p.m. up freight from Evercreech Junction.

8th July, 1958

MIDFORD

In addition to crossing over the Bath road, Cam Brook and Somerset Coal Canal, Midford viaduct also carried the S & D over the Great Western Limpley Stoke – Camerton branch. For years I had hoped one day to get a picture of an S & D train crossing over the viaduct whilst at the same time, a Great Western train was passing underneath. However, by 1958 it was obvious I was not going to get this, because the G.W. line was no longer in use and a start had been made on lifting the track.

One Saturday morning whilst having a cup of tea with signalman Percy Savage in Midford box, we saw the Great Western demolition train pass by, and I mentioned my 'lost dream' to Percy. To my delighted surprise Percy suddenly said, "Oh, I think I might be able to fix it for you for a couple of pints". It turned out that Percy knew the enginemen engaged on the track-lifting work.

Early the following week, my 'phone rang in my office. It was Percy. "I have fixed it, Mr. Peters. Wednesday for the 11 o'clock down goods. That O.K.?" On occasions like this, one can't expect everything to be just right, and Wednesday morning was miserable, misty and damp. But when I got to Midford at 11 o'clock, there, sure enough, was the Great Western train, drawn up just to the west of the viaduct – and I got my picture!

It only remains to add that it was with the greatest pleasure I handed over the funds to Percy for the S & D/G.W.R. gathering at the Hope and Anchor that evening.

172. A dream realised! – B.R. class 5 No. 73116 passing over Midford viaduct with the 11.00 a.m. Bath – Evercreech Junction goods, whilst Pannier Tank No. 9628 stands below on the G.W.R. Limpley Stoke – Camerton branch with the demolition train.

30th June, 1958

171. At the beginning of 1958 the parapets on Midford viaduct were rebuilt, most of the work being done on Sundays when no regular traffic ran over the S & D between Bath and Evercreech Junction. In this picture the bricks from the demolished old parapets are being loaded into an engineers' train.

5th January, 1958

THE S & D 4F 0-6-0s

In 1958 all five 4F 0-6-0s, built for the S & D.J.R. in 1922 by Armstrong Whitworth & Co., were going strong and continuing to be used as 'Maids of all work'.

173. (Right) With the Midford valley looking its best on a lovely summer's afternoon, S & D 4F No. 44559 stands at Midford Up Outer Home signal with the 1.10 p.m. up goods from Evercreech Junction, waiting for the single-line section into Bath Junction to become clear.

31st May, 1958

174. (Below) S & D 4F No. 44558 and 7F No. 53810 running down past the grounds of Midford Castle with the 7.35 a.m. (SO) Nottingham to Bournemouth.

28th June, 1958

MIDSOMER NORTON

This attractive station was typical of the style used by the S & D on their Bath extension. The 1 in 50 grade up to Midsomer Norton eased off to 1 in 300 through the platforms, only to set in again at 1 in 53 immediately south of the station.

175. 2P No. 40568 and S.R. Pacific No. 34107 "Blandford Forum" coasting down the bank towards Midsomer Norton with the up "Pines Express". The crew of the Pacific are driver Donald Beale and fireman Peter Smith. Most unusually, the 2P is carrying the normal B.R. express headlamp code, instead of the S & D's own distinctive code for a passenger train of one lamp beneath the chimney and one over the left hand buffer. (On gaining control of the S & D, the Western Region had issued an edict that B.R. standard headlamp codes would be used — but S & D enginemen viewed this instruction with the 'Nelson touch'.)

7th June, 1958

176. The 9.10 a.m. (SO) Birmingham to Bournemouth (12 noon off Bath) coming up through the station, hauled by 4F No. 44167 and B.R. class 5 No. 73051.

6th September, 1958

177. Whilst shunting in Norton Hill colliery yard, N.C.B. 0-6-0 saddle tank "Lord Salisbury", meets 'Jinty' 0-6-0T. No. 47557 propelling in some empty wagons off a down freight train.

19th April, 1958

NORTON HILL COLLIERY

Most collieries around Radstock were shunted by B.R., but at Norton Hill the National Coal Board provided their own locomotives.

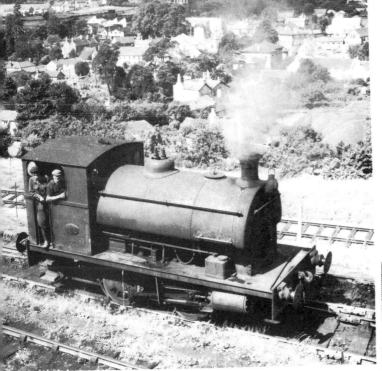

178. The crew of this small N.C.B. 0-4-0 saddle tank, kindly halted their shunting for a moment so that I could get this picture of them with Midsomer Norton as the back-cloth. This engine, built by Peckett & Sons Ltd. in 1929, came to Norton Hill Colliery in 1950.

15th August, 1958

179. N.C.B. 0-6-0ST. "Lord Salisbury", built by Peckett & Sons Ltd., Bristol, in 1906.

LOCOMOTIVE VARIETY

In 1958 the variety of motive power on the S & D was as great as ever. The pictures on this page are of two types of class 4 locomotives working over the line. Both views also show Midford's tall, stately Down Advance Starting signal, destined to be replaced by a much shorter, commonplace Western Region type.

180. Pulling away from Midford — ex-L.M.S. 4F 0-6-0 No. 44417 with the 3.20 p.m. down stopping train from Bath to Templecombe.

3rd May, 1958

181. B.R. standard class 4 2-6-0 No. 76066 an Eastleigh engine — coasting down the 1 in 60 towards Midford with the 1.10 p.m. up stopping train from Bournemouth West to Bristol, Temple Meads.

26th May, 1958

182. The up "Pines", drawn by 2P No. 40569 and S.R. Pacific No. 34107 "Blandford Forum", coming in over Bath Junction on a bright winter's morning near the end of the year.
27th December, 1958

— AND EVEN "THE PINES EXPRESS" PRODUCED INTERESTING VARIATIONS IN MOTIVE POWER

183. Two B.R. standard 4-6-0s, class 4 No. 75072 and class 5 No. 73047, running in to Bath with the up "Pines".
17th May, 1958

184. 3F No. 43194, old S & D.J.R. No. 62 built at Derby in 1896, draws near to Wyke Champflower with the 2.20 p.m. local from Highbridge to Templecombe.

2nd August, 1958

VETERAN EX-S & D.J.R.
3F 0-6-0s

185. Late in the evening of an August Saturday, 3F No. 43248, piloting 7F No. 53804, comes storming through Shepton Mallet with a heavy north-bound empty pigeon special. 43248, originally No. 75, was built for the S & D.J.R. by Neilson Reid & Co. in 1902.

23rd August, 1958

186. 7F No. 53801, piloted by 4F No. 44523, climbs towards Binegar with a pigeon special of 14 bogies.

23rd August, 1958

PIGEON SPECIALS

Each year the S & D handled a substantial number of pigeon specials which came down from the Midlands and the North. As the pigeon racing season progressed, so the birds were carried further down the line to give them a longer flight home. In high summer Templecombe was frequently chosen as the location for the pigeons' release.

Pigeon specials, which normally ran on Saturdays, were heavy trains, and motive power over the S & D was invariably a 7F 2-8-0, with assistance being given for the climb over the Mendips.

187. The empty pigeon specials did not normally set off on the return run north until late in the afternoon, when the main flow of passenger traffic was over. On a fine Saturday evening in early September, S & D 7F No. 53807 is coming through the Wyke curves with a 16-bogie empty pigeon special which had left Templecombe at 6.45 p.m. 53807 is running tender-first because the 7Fs were too long to be turned on Templecombe's balance-type turntable. A stop would be made at Evercreech Junction for 53807 to be turned on the table by the North box and a 4F attached as pilot for the climb over the Mendips.

6th September, 1958

INTERESTING VISITORS

The graceful ex-L & S.W.R. T9 4-4-0s were not used regularly over the S & D. Every now and again, however, one made a welcome appearance, standing in for a booked engine that had failed.

188.
Bath, Green Park, at dusk. (Note platform lamp burning brightly!) Ex-L & S.W.R. T9 4-4-0 No. 30310 is about to depart at 7:05 p.m. with the 6.02 p.m. Bristol, Temple Meads, to Bournemouth West. The T9 had worked up from Bournemouth on the 1.10 p.m., having been substituted at short notice by Bournemouth shed for the usual B.R. class 4 which had failed.
17th April, 1958

189. — And just over a week later, it happened again! Another T9, this time No. 30706, appeared on the S & D once more as a result of the sudden failure of a B.R. class 4 on the 1.10 p.m. up from Bournemouth. British Summer Time having just started, it was light enough to follow and photograph this T9 as far as Binegar on her run south with the 7.05 p.m. off Bath. She is seen here about to stop at Midsomer Norton.

26th April, 1958

Towards the end of July T9 No. 30120 spent a week on the S & D, on loan to Templecombe shed from Eastleigh M.P.D. Sadly I was in London on business for the whole of this week, and knew nothing of the T9's visit until I came face to face with her on Bath shed on the Saturday morning.

190. T9 No. 30120 on Bath shed on the Saturday morning at the end of her week's stay on the S & D. This is the T9 which has been preserved. Beautifully restored in L & S.W.R. livery, she may be seen at the National Railway Museum at York.

26th July, 1958

191. On the Saturday afternoon, T9 No. 30120 left Bath for her own shed, Eastleigh (71A), attached as pilot to S.R. Pacific No. 34041 "Wilton" on the 7.35 a.m. (SO) Nottingham to Bournemouth. The pair are seen here coming up to Masbury Summit with their train.

26th July, 1958

192. A 'bird's-eye' view of Bath M.P.D. In the foreground is the old S & D shed which was largely constructed of wood, had four roads and could hold 18 engines. The roof of the much smaller, stone-built ex-Midland shed can just be seen behind the coaling stage, whilst in the middle distance is Bath, Green Park, station. The brick-built coaling stage was erected in 1953/4, to replace an earlier wooden stage built in 1884.
21st June, 1958

BATH MOTIVE POWER DEPOT

193.
Inside the S & D shed, showing the timber trussed roof. Keeping 2P No. 40698 company are two London Midland Region engines, "Jubilee" No. 45701 "Conqueror", and Caprotti 'Black Five' No. 44749, resting before their booked return journeys to the North.
21st June, 1958

194. 2Ps standing outside the old Midland shed. The engines visible are Nos. 40568, 40698, 40511 and 40563, with B.R. class 5 No. 73050 on the right.

24th May, 1958

195. (Right) An interesting visitor, B.R. Caprotti class 5 No. 73143 from shed 16A, Nottingham, Southwell, waiting to take over the 10.05 a.m. (SO) from Bournemouth for the continuation of the run up to Derby.

21st June, 1958

196. (Below) On the first Saturday in August – the busiest day of the year for the S & D – three Horwich 'Crabs', Nos. 42799, 42921 and 42782 and a 'Black Five', are lined up outside the Midland shed, waiting to take over trains for the North.

2nd August, 1958

197. S & D 7F No. 53800 — the doyen of the class — running south over Cole viaduct with the 7.43 a.m. (SO) Birmingham, New Street, to Bournemouth West.

2nd August, 1958

THE S & D 7F 2-8-0s ON PASSENGER TRAINS

Eight years had now passed since it first became necessary to make limited use of the S & D 7Fs for hauling passenger trains — and 1958 saw no lessening of the necessity for their use on Saturdays at the height of the summer service.

198. Another view of the 7.43 a.m. (SO) from Birmingham, this time coasting down past the grounds of Midford Castle, hauled by 7F No. 53808 with 4F No. 44523 coupled ahead of her. The 4F was working down to Evercreech Junction in order to assist an up express, and was diagrammed to be coupled to the 10.32 a.m. off Bath (7.43 a.m. (SO) ex-Birmingham) to avoid having to arrange a light engine path for her. As the 7.43 a.m. (SO) from Birmingham ran non-stop through Evercreech Junction, the 4F came off at Shepton Mallet, the first booked stop of this express, and then followed on down to the Junction, light engine.

30th August, 1958

199. — And our Birmingham friend again, this time swinging through the curves south of Wellow. On this occasion the 7F was No. 53809 and the 4F coupled ahead of her was ex-S & D No. 44559.

6th September, 1958

200. The 2.45 p.m. (SO) Bournemouth to Bristol climbing past Prestleigh. The train engine is a 'borrowed' 'Black Five', No. 45332, assisted by 7F No. 53808.

30th August, 1958

201. 2P No. 40698 and 7F No. 53801 with the 12-coach 9.10 a.m. (SO) Birmingham to Bournemouth (12 noon off Bath) climbing towards Moorewood.

30th August, 1958

TRACK TEST SPECIAL

The Western Region start to assert their authority — the S & D's track is subjected to a test run. (For the record, track maintenance on the Somerset and Dorset was exemplary. Although the line between Bath and Evercreech Junction abounded in curves, the riding was remarkably smooth.)

202. B.R. standard class 5 No. 73051 making a rapid climb up the 1 in 50 bank out of Bath with the light-weight four-coach special. Note that with Western Region officers on board the train, the S & D footplate crew were 'playing it safe' and had put up the B.R. express headlamp code on their engine!
13th May, 1958

203. The track-testing train about to be swallowed up by Devonshire Tunnel. A high-speed run had been scheduled for the special. Three of the test engineers could be seen looking out from the rear of the test coach. The one on the left appeared to be saying his prayers!
13th May, 1958

INSPECTION SPECIAL

Towards the end of the year the general manager of the Western Region, Mr. K.W.C. Grand, made a tour of inspection of his new acquisition. The special started from Temple Meads, Bristol, and ran down the Western main line to Highbridge, where it joined the S & D. The route then followed was — Highbridge, Evercreech Junction, Templecombe (Reverse), Evercreech Junction, Bath and, over the Midland, back to Temple Meads.

The two-coach special was worked throughout by an S & D engine, 2P 4-4-0 No. 40700 — and once again the S & D footplate crew had been careful to put up the B.R. express headlamp code on their engine!

204. (Above) The special climbing through Horsecombe Vale in the late afternoon.

205. (Right) — and about to enter Combe Down Tunnel.

29th October, 1958

206. On a very gloomy afternoon in late December, two ex-Great Western engines, 0-6-0 No. 2215 and pannier tank No. 3604, cross Midford viaduct on their way back to Bath after taking part in clearance trials down the line.

23rd December, 1958

207. The pannier tank, No. 3604, standing outside the Midland shed at dusk after her arrival back in Bath. The two ex-Great Western engines remained at Bath for a short while before proceeding back to their home sheds.

23rd December, 1958

208. Earlier in December a Western Region 'WD' class 8F 2-8-0, No. 90693, had been sent over to the S & D to carry out clearance tests down the line. The engine is seen here engaged in these tests at Wellow.

9th December, 1958

209.
By the end of 1958 it was clear that Western Region locomotives would be coming to the S & D. So the last picture for this year is a look back to Templecombe, prior to the penetration of this depot by ex-Great Western engines. In the foreground are ex-S.R. G6 class 0-6-0T. No. 30274, ex-S & D.J.R. 2P 4-4-0 No. 40634 and ex-Midland class 3F 0-6-0 No. 43436. Just visible in the distance, S & D 7F 2-8-0 No. 53802 stands half on the turntable — which was too short to turn her!

1st March, 1958

210.
The first run over the S & D by a rebuilt Bulleid Light Pacific. No. 34039 "Boscastle", after arriving in Bath with the up "Pines Express", waits for the turntable to become free. The Pacific's fireman, leaning out of the cab enjoying the summer sunshine, is Alan Northover.
19th June, 1959

1959

And so we come to 1959, the last year of the 'Fifties. With the Somerset and Dorset now under the control of the Western Region, ex-G.W.R. engines were introduced onto the line with varying degrees of success. With the intention of dispensing with the elderly S & D 7F 2-8-0s (which incidentally had a higher tractive effort than the ex-G.W.R. 28XX 2-8-0s) an 'Austerity' 8F 2-8-0 was brought over from Bristol for a test run with the 11.00 a.m. down goods to Evercreech Junction. Descending the southern slopes of the Mendips, the engine's brake power proved inadequate, and the train ran away. But of course an 'Austerity' was not a Swindon engine, so next an ex-G.W.R. 56XX class 0-6-2T. was sent over to work the morning coal train from Midsomer Norton to Bath. The 0-6-2T. faired no better than the 'Austerity' 2-8-0, for her brakes were also unable to control the train, which ran away. What the Western Region authorities had apparently failed to appreciate, was that the S & D 7F 2-8-0s probably had the most efficient brake power of any freight locomotive on British Railways. Neither the 'Austerity' 2-8-0 nor the ex-G.W.R. 0-6-2T. was seen again on the S & D – but on the other hand, ex-G.W.R. pannier tanks did take over with success, the shunting of Bath goods yards.

On a happier note, 1959 saw the first appearance over the Somerset and Dorset of a rebuilt Bulleid Light Pacific (Bournemouth shed continuing to help out with motive power on summer Saturdays). Initially, the Western Region laid down a 50 m.p.h. speed limit on these engines, but S & D enginemen tended to view this instruction with the 'Nelson touch'!

211. 0-4-4T. No. 58086, the last Johnson tank on the S & D. After being taken out of service, the engine was brought from Highbridge up to Bath shed, where she spent her remaining months in store, tucked away behind the water softening plant.
5th December, 1959

212. S & D 7F 2-8-0 No. 53800, the first of the class to be built, and the first to be withdrawn. 53800, originally S & D.J.R. No. 80, was built at Derby in 1914, entering service in March of that year. She was taken out of service on 3rd June, 1959, and on 15th June left on her final journey to Works to be broken up. This was my last picture of her, taken at Masbury Halt on a Sunday when she was working an engineers' train.
15th March, 1959

213. S & D 7F No. 53809 hurrying along west of Wellow with the 12.35 p.m. down freight from Bath.

28th February, 1959

THE S & D 7F 2-8-0s

Although the first of the S & D 7Fs was withdrawn in June, the remaining ten engines in the class continued to give excellent service on both freight and passenger trains.

214. S.R. Pacific No. 34102 "Lapford", piloted by 7F No. 53807, emerges from Devonshire Tunnel and coasts down the bank into Bath with the 11.12 a.m. (SO) Bournemouth to Sheffield.

15th August, 1959

THE FIRST — AND LAST — RUN OF A 'WD' CLASS 8F 2-8-0 OVER THE S & D

Early in January the Western Region arranged for the trial over the S & D of a 'WD' class 8F 2-8-0. The train selected for the run was the 11.00 a.m. Bath — Evercreech Junction goods and this was specially made up for the test and included six vacuum fitted vans next to the engine to be used in case of emergency during the braking tests down the southern slopes of the Mendips.

The descent from Masbury Summit down to Shepton Mallet, where the engine was booked to take water, was pretty hectic, but with the aid of the rising grade from Charlton viaduct up into the station, they just managed to pull up beside the water column. The Western Region locomotive inspector, who had never ridden over the line before, turned to the driver and remarked "Well, that went off all right then" — not realising that the real test was yet to come with the 5-mile descent down to Evercreech Junction, which included over three miles of 1 in 50!

Off they set, gingerly, from Shepton Mallet, but by Prestleigh speed was building up at an alarming rate and the engine no longer had control of the train. Somewhat disturbed, the inspector called out to the driver, "Will you be able to pull up by the Junction, driver?" To which he got the very abrupt reply "Junction be b . . . . .! We will be b . . . . . lucky if we have stopped by Cole!" Whereupon the vacuum fitted vans were hastily brought into action — and the 'Austerity' 8Fs were not seen again on the S & D.

215. The engine used for the test, No. 90125, should have worked the 11.00 a.m. down goods on the Wednesday, 21st January, but disgraced herself by going off the boil shortly before departure time! She was ignominiously removed back to the shed by S & D 7F No. 53804, which then took the train down to Evercreech Junction.

21st January, 1959

216. 'WD' class 8F 2-8-0 No. 90125 pounding up the bank out of Bath with the 11.00 a.m. Bath — Evercreech Junction goods. Note the six vacuum-fitted vans next to the engine.

22nd January, 1959

THE FIRST RUN OVER THE S & D BY A REBUILT BULLEID LIGHT PACIFIC

A rebuilt Bulleid "West Country" Pacific appeared on the S & D scene for the first time on Friday, 19th June, when No. 34039 "Boscastle" worked the up and down "Pines Express".

217. No. 34039 "Boscastle" drifts down off the S & D and over Bath Junction with the up "Pines Express". It might seem surprising that although the Pacific had only 8 on, she was provided with a pilot, 2P No. 40569, from Evercreech Junction up to Bath. The pilot engine for "The Pines Express" was a Templecombe shed working. Although on this occasion the up train was within the maximum load limit for a Bulleid Light Pacific, the down "Pines" in the afternoon was known to be a heavy train which would require an assisting engine. So the sensible way of working the 2P up to Bath for the down 'Pines Assisting' turn in the afternoon, was to couple her ahead of the Pacific on the morning 'up' run.

19th June, 1959

218. "Boscastle" about to be turned. The positioning of a Bulleid Light Pacific with a wheelbase of 57 ft. 6 in. and an overall length of 67 ft. 4¾ in., on Bath's 60' turntable called for care and precision. Because of the considerable overhang, if the engine was positioned just a shade too far forward, then as the turning proceeded, the front buffers would foul wagons standing on the coal stage road (seen on the right of this picture).

19th June, 1959

219. The return run in the afternoon. 2P No. 40569 and rebuilt S.R. Pacific No. 34039 "Boscastle" leaving Midford viaduct with the down "Pines Express".
19th June, 1959

THE HIGHBRIDGE—
TEMPLECOMBE SERVICE

The last of the Johnson tanks having finally vanished from the S & D scene, the Highbridge — Templecombe service was now in the hands of the Ivatt 2-6-2 tanks and Johnson 3F 0-6-0s.

220. The morning train — 9.45 a.m. off Highbridge — climbing up through Pylle woods, hauled by Ivatt 2-6-2T. No. 41296.
27th June, 1959

221. (Below) Johnson 3F 0-6-0 No. 43216 — old S & D.J.R. No. 72 built by Neilson Reid & Co. in 1902 — nearing Wincanton with the 2.20 p.m. Highbridge — Templecombe local.
5th September, 1959

222. 4F No. 44559 and 7F No. 53807 nearing Evercreech Junction with their train of 21 bogies. Because the 7Fs were too long for Templecombe's turntable, 53807 had to start her return journey, tender-first. However, a stop was about to be made at Evercreech Junction for her to be turned on the table by the North box.

16th May, 1959

PIGEON SPECIAL

In the early hours of Saturday morning, 16th May, one of the longest trains ever run over the S & D, a pigeon special of 21 bogies, was taken down to Templecombe by two 7F 2-8-0s. The return run of the empty train in the evening was also scheduled for two 7Fs but, most disappointingly, Templecombe replaced one with a 4F!

223. After the 7F had been turned at Evercreech Junction, the two engines set off on the mammoth task of hauling their immense train up the 8-mile climb to Masbury Summit, 811 feet above sea level. They are seen here, plodding up towards Evercreech New.

16th May, 1959

224. The train had been brought down to Bath from the Midlands in the early hours of the morning by two ex-Great Western engines, 2-6-0s Nos. 6348 and 5330. They are seen here, spending a quiet day inside the S & D shed at Bath before taking over the train in the evening for the return run north.

16th May, 1959

EVERCREECH JUNCTION

The starting point for the 8-mile ascent to Masbury Summit, and where all up trains of over 8 coaches – unless hauled by an S & D 7F – had an assisting engine attached for the climb over the Mendips.

225. Five pilot engines – all 2Ps – lined up on a stormy Saturday morning in high summer, waiting to assist up expresses over the Mendips.

27th June, 1959

226. S & D 7F 2-8-0 No. 53804, ready to leave the Up yard with the 3.20 p.m. goods for Bath.

30th May, 1959

227. B.R. class 4 2-6-0 No. 76067, running in with the 1.10 p.m. Bournemouth West to Bristol, Temple Meads, crosses rebuilt S.R. Pacific No. 34039 "Boscastle", standing in the down loop with the 7.35 a.m. (SO) Nottingham to Bournemouth West.
22nd August, 1959

STURMINSTER NEWTON

On the 16-mile single line section between Temple-combe and Blandford Forum.

228.
With the single line now clear, "Boscastle" gets the road and sets off south with her train. The crew of the Pacific are driver Jim Tranter and fireman Alan Northover.

22nd August, 1959

STURMINSTER NEWTON

229. B.R. class 5 No. 73049 rumbles over the river bridge north of Sturminster Newton with the 7.42 a.m. (SO) Birmingham, New Street, to Bournemouth West.

22nd August, 1959

CROSSING THE RIVER STOUR

230. The 11.12 a.m. (SO) Bournemouth West to Sheffield, hauled by B.R. class 5 No. 73028, crosses over the River Stour just south of Blandford Forum station.

22nd August, 1959

BLANDFORD FORUM

231. S.R. Pacific No. 34041 "Wilton" crosses over the River Stour with the 11.40 a.m. (SO) Bournemouth West to Derby.

22nd August, 1959

STURMINSTER NEWTON

232. 'Jinty' 0-6-0T. No. 47342 passing over the river as she ambles northwards from Sturminster Newton with a pick-up goods.

9th October, 1959

233. S.R. Pacific No. 34043 "Combe Martin" and B.R. class 5 No. 73051 leaving Midford viaduct with the down "Pines Express". The train has just come to the end of the 4-mile single line section from Bath Junction and is running on to double track which would now last for the next 32 miles down to Templecombe.

27th June, 1959

B.R. 5s AND S.R. PACIFICS IN 'DOUBLE-HARNESS'

234. B.R. class 5 No. 73051 and rebuilt S.R. Pacific No. 34028 "Eddystone" climbing up the 1 in 60 away from Midford with the down "Pines". The crew of the Pacific are driver Donald Beale and fireman Peter Smith.

3rd August, 1959

235. The down "Pines Express" running through the Midford valley south of Twinhoe, drawn by B.R. class 5 No. 73028 and S.R. Pacific No. 34044 "Woolacombe".

18th May, 1959

236. — And a couple of B.R. 4-6-0s together. Late in the afternoon of a lovely summer's day, class 5 No. 73019 and class 4 No. 75072 come sweeping through the curves past Midford's Up Distant signal with the 2.45 p.m. (SO) Bournemouth West to Bristol, Temple Meads.

18th July, 1959

237. The exciting and very rare spectacle of two S & D 7F 2-8-0s on a passenger train – something I saw only six times in 40 years. Two of the 1914 series engines, Nos. 53804 and 53802, come storming up the 1 in 50 bank out of Bath with the 7.35 a.m. (SO) Nottingham to Bournemouth. (A *very* rapid car chase followed, resulting in a second picture of this train nearing Chilcompton – picture 96 in my book "The Somerset and Dorset – An English Cross-Country Railway.")

4th July, 1959

THE S & D 7F 2-8-0s ON PASSENGER TRAINS

For the summer service in 1959 the S & D had available more B.R. Standard class locomotives than ever before, together with, of course, a large stud of 4-4-0s and 0-6-0s. As in previous years, Bournemouth shed also co-operated with liberal lending of S.R. Pacifics for use over the S & D on Saturdays. Yet all this motive power was insufficient to deal with the volume of traffic that passed over the line on Saturdays at the height of the summer service, and once again limited use had to be made of the faithful old S & D 7F 2-8-0s.

238. On a hot, cloudless afternoon in late August, S & D 7F No. 53807 and S.R. Pacific No. 34040 "Crewkerne" climb towards Masbury Summit with the 10.28 a.m. (SO) Manchester, London Road, to Bournemouth West.
22nd August, 1959

239. S & D 7F No. 53804 takes water during the booked stop at Shepton Mallet with the 7.42 a.m. (SO) Birmingham, New Street, to Bournemouth West. From Shepton Mallet this express then ran non-stop to Wincanton, so having the distinction of being the only train not scheduled to call at Evercreech Junction. Standing on the right is 4F No. 44424 which was on her way to Evercreech Junction to assist an up express over the Mendips. The 4F had worked down to Shepton Mallet, coupled ahead of the 7F, and as soon as the express had departed, she would follow on down to Evercreech Junction, light engine.
20th June, 1959

240. S & D 7F No. 53802 standing in Midford station with a Sunday engineers' train. The unusual flat roof of Midford signal box came about as a result of the rebuilding of the box in 1936 after it had been damaged in an accident.
8th November, 1959

241. (Below) Early morning at Midford. 4F No. 44424, running in over the viaduct with the 7.00 a.m. up local from Templecombe, was not fitted with a tablet catcher and the signalman is holding up the 'big pouch' for the fireman to take by hand.

29th August, 1959

242. After coming to a stand to give up the single-line token, the 7-car DMU forming a Whit Sunday excursion from Birmingham, sets off again over Midford viaduct on the run down to Bournemouth.

17th May, 1959

243. (Below) On a bright but windy afternoon in late March, B.R. class 4 4-6-0 No. 75071 leaves the viaduct and starts the 1 in 60 climb away from Midford with the 4.37 p.m. Bath — Templecombe stopping train.

28th March, 1959

244. 2P No. 40652 and rebuilt S.R. Pacific No. 34039 "Boscastle" swinging through the reverse curves towards Midford with the up "Pines Express".

20th June, 1959

THE MIDFORD VALLEY

245. The view from the rear brake van as the 12.35 p.m. down goods runs through the Midford valley towards Wellow. (The second brake van was put on by B.R. to carry members of the Bath Railway Society on an expedition down to Evercreech Junction and back – a most enjoyable 'outing'.)

26th September, 1959

246.
Although the S & D no longer had any 'Black Fives' of their own, they took every opportunity to 'borrow' one whenever possible! No. 44813, a 21A Saltley engine, having arrived in Bath on the Friday with a perishables, was quickly 'tucked away' behind the water softening plant — and here she is on the Saturday afternoon passing Midford's Down Advance Starter, on her way down to Bournemouth with a Bank Holiday relief from the North.

16th May, 1959

247.
2P No. 40563 and B.R. class 5 No. 73019 are held at Midford's Up Outer Home signal with the 10.05 a.m. (SO) Bournemouth to Derby, waiting for the single-line section into Bath Junction, whilst coming by, heading south, is the train which had been occupying the section, the 7.35 a.m. (SO) Nottingham to Bournemouth, hauled by 4F No. 44269 and B.R. class 5 No. 73116.

20th June, 1959

248. S.R. Pacific No. 34044 "Woolacombe" piloted by elderly ex-Midland Railway 2P 4-4-0 No. 40537, comes in over Bath Junction with the up "Pines Express". On the right, S & D 7F No. 53809 is drifting back onto a down goods with which she will set off for Evercreech Junction at 12.35 p.m.

4th April, 1959

BATH JUNCTION

249. Although, since the Western Region had gained control of the Somerset & Dorset, "The Pines Express" was no longer worked south of Bath by 'Black Fives', the London Midland Region often used one of these most competent locomotives for hauling the express north of Bath. On the first Saturday in January the London Midland Region had a 'Black Five' at Bath with no return working, so it was coupled ahead of the "Pines" 'Black Five'. The two engines, Nos. 44776 and 44818, made a dramatic departure from Bath with the "Pines" and are seen here passing Bath Junction, half a mile out from the terminus, in fine style.

3rd January, 1959

250. On Christmas Eve the up "Pines Express", hauled by S.R. Pacific No. 34028 "Eddystone", arrived at Evercreech Junction to find no assisting engine waiting for her – a relief to Sheffield, running ahead of the "Pines", had had to take it! A 'Jinty' tank was hastily summoned from Radstock to pilot the Pacific over the Mendips as far as Binegar, and Bath despatched another 'Jinty', No. 47496, out to Wellow to assist in the climb up through Combe Down Tunnel and into Bath. In this picture the 'Jinty' and the Pacific are seen coming in over Bath Junction with the up "Pines". I appreciate that this photograph has been reproduced before, but I felt the year 1959 would not be really complete without it.

24th December, 1959

251.
Bath Gasworks was situated on the north side of the line at Bath Junction, and the vast bulk of the towering gasometers formed the back-cloth to many of my pictures taken at this location. To shunt their extensive network of sidings, the Gas Board had two small saddle tanks, and whenever I was taking photographs at Bath Junction, I always hoped there might be the opportunity to obtain a picture of one of these attractive little engines standing alongside an S & D 7F 2-8-0. But it was not to be. The small gasworks engines were most elusive, and often all one saw of them was a tantalising column of steam rising above a building, or a wispy trail of smoke passing behind a rake of wagons. In this picture, taken outside their shed on a Saturday morning, the engine on the left was built by the Avonside Engine Co. in 1928, whilst the smaller engine is a Peckett of 1912.

21st March, 1959

252.   4F No. 44146, Caprotti 5 No. 44754, Horwich 'Crab' No. 42748 and 'Black Five' No. 44826, pose outside the old Midland shed.
3rd August, 1959

BATH MOTIVE POWER DEPOT

An interesting variety of engines 'on shed'.

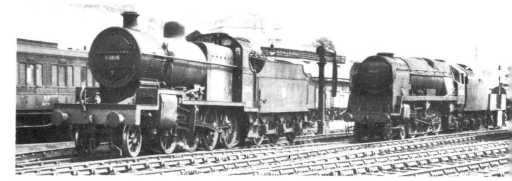

253.   S & D 7F No. 53806 and rebuilt Bulleid Pacific No. 34028 "Eddystone".
3rd August, 1959

254.   Rebuilt Bulleid Pacific No. 34039 "Boscastle", being turned, faces 2P No. 40564 and B.R. class 5 No. 73051.
19th June, 1959

BATH, GREEN PARK, STATION

— MORNING

255. B.R. class 3 2-6-2T. No. 82041 – immaculate in lined-out green livery – about to set off over the Midland line with a local for Bristol, Temple Meads. 82041, one of the Western Region's transfers to Bath M.P.D., was frequently used on the 6.05 p.m. (SX) Bath – Binegar local (leaving Binegar at 7.10 p.m. on the return run to Bath).

28th February, 1959

— NOON

256. S & D 7Fs Nos. 53804 and 53802 prepare to leave Bath with the 7.35 a.m. (SO) Nottingham to Bournemouth (Bath arr. 12.05 p.m., dep. 12.24 p.m.).

This was the penultimate occasion on which two S & D 7F 2-8-0s were used together to work a passenger train. The very last time was on Saturday, 15th August, 1959.

4th July, 1959

— AND NIGHT

257. The end of the day. 2P No. 40564 waits to leave with the last train of the day, the 10.25 p.m. down to Templecombe.

9th September, 1959

S & D SIGNALS

Although the Western Region had made a start at replacing old signals with their own modern type, as 1959 drew to a close, many elderly S & D signals still survived. These two attractive examples were at Evercreech Junction.

258. This bracket signal stood near the entrance to the Up yard. The left hand arm was the Up Branch Home, and the right hand arm, the Up Main Home. The subsidiary arm lower down the post was — to use the words of the official locking chart — the Shunt to Highbridge Line signal.

26th September, 1959

259. An S & D Backing signal. Down freights arriving at Evercreech Junction came to a stand on the main line. A shunting engine would then couple on to the rear of the train, and it was this 'Calling Back arm' which authorised the shunting engine driver to draw the train back off the main line and onto the branch, from where it could be propelled into the Up yard.

26th September, 1959

260. Trespassing on the Somerset and Dorset was not encouraged!

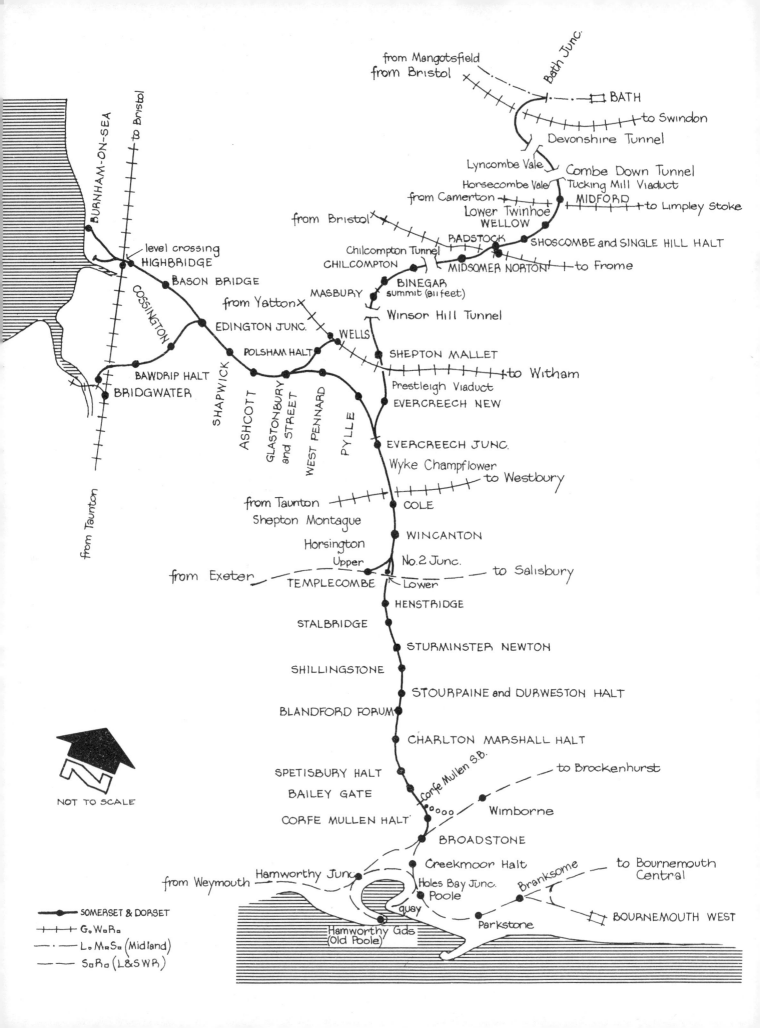